A SOUND *Mind*

THE POWER OF THE HOLY SPIRIT TO HEAL AND DELIVER FROM EVIL SPIRITS

By

SHANNESE DAVIDSON

A SOUND MIND

The Power of the Holy Spirit to Heal and Deliver from Evil Spirits

Copyright © 2024 by Shannese Davidson & Take Flight Publishing. All rights reserved.

All Scripture quotations, unless otherwise indicated, are taken from the Holy Bible, New King James Version. Copyright © 1982 by Thomas Nelson, Inc. Used by permission.

All rights reserved. No portion of this book may be reproduced in any form without permission from the publisher, except as permitted by U.S. copyright law. For permission contact: shannese77@gmail.com

www.takeflightpublishing.org

Dedication

I want to dedicate this book to my family, especially my mother, persons who are struggling with mental illness, and all those who support and care for individuals with mental illnesses.

Family, friends, and community support are crucial for recovery and mental health maintenance.

Those who suffer from mental illnesses are not "mad" or "insane."

You are ~~not~~ strong enough.
You are ~~not~~ good enough.
You are ~~not~~ smart enough.
You are ~~not~~ brave enough.
You are ~~not~~ beautiful enough.
You are ~~not~~ kind enough.
God made you enough.
Because you are enough!

Acknowledgements

I would like to express heartfelt gratitude to the triune God—God the Father, my Lord and Savior, Jesus Christ of Nazareth, and the precious Holy Spirit. I thank the Holy Trinity for His tender mercies, unmerited favor, and abounding grace. I thank Him for turning a situation that the enemy meant for evil for my good. I thank Him for giving me the opportunity and guidance to share my testimony and journey of His healing and deliverance power that He performed in my life.

In late 2023, I shared my testimony with Jason Mills, also known as JayQues, an author and a friend. His immediate response was that I had a powerful testimony to share. He asked me if I had ever considered putting my experience in a book. He encouraged me to pray about it and offered to guide me through the process once I received confirmation from the Holy Spirit. Jason has been a constant support and motivator throughout this process. I thank Jason for devoting his time and resources, obeying the Holy Spirit, and guiding me to make my book successful and to share my testimony with the world.

Acknowledgements

I want to thank Minister Knight for her visitation to my church, Ebenezer Open Bible Church, as our guest speaker at our Pastor's appreciation on December 31, 2023, and for obeying the Holy Spirit. After I expressed my penned appreciation to my pastor in the service, Minister Knight called me privately. She said, "Do you know you have the gift of writing? When are you going to start writing your book?" Surprised as the Holy Spirit confirmed that I should write this memoir, I replied, "I'm thinking about it." She responded, "You need to stop thinking. You must start writing next year (which would have been the next day)."

I want to thank Reverend Windel Daley for his enthusiastic support and encouragement when I first mentioned writing a book and throughout the writing process. His constant prayers and unwavering support as my pastor and friend have been a source of strength and motivation. I am thankful that he allowed the Holy Spirit to use him as a vessel from the beginning of my journey. Thank you for being there for me throughout this journey.

I want to thank Apostle Christina Williams from the Way of Holiness Deliverance Ministry and her family for the love and kindness they have shown me. Thank you, Christina, for your encouragement and motivation to write this book. I am so grateful that you have allowed the Holy Spirit to use you as a vessel.

I am deeply grateful to my family, especially my mother, for their unwavering support and encouragement throughout my journey and while writing this book. Thank you for surrounding me with the love and support I solemnly needed and for not giving up on me at any point in life. Thank you for not treating me less than a person in the past, for always believing in me, for never seeing me as a burden or disappointment, and for being there for me until God gave me the breakthrough I solemnly needed. I couldn't ask for a better family; I appreciate you all.

I also would like to express gratitude to those who have been there for me throughout the ordeal—extended family, friends, church family, healthcare professionals, and even strangers who have helped. I appreciate all your support and encouragement. Thank you!

May God continue to bless and keep you all in Jesus' name.

Dedication	i
Acknowledgements	iii
Introduction	1
CHAPTER 1: Early Life	17
CHAPTER 2: A Prey In The Enemy's Trap	27
CHAPTER 3: Birthday Gone Wrong	39
CHAPTER 4: Hospital Visitation	45
CHAPTER 5: Power of the Mind	71
CHAPTER 6: Spiritual Warfare – Efforts To Destroy Our "Stars"	97
CHAPTER 7: Journey of Mental Deliverance & Healing	115
EPILOGUE: Overcoming Stigma Attached to Mental Illness	137
AFFIRMATIONS: Declaration of Truth	165
Prayer for Those Struggling with Mental Illnesses	169
Prayer of Salvation	171
References	173

Introduction

Life's journey is filled with trials, struggles, tribulations, beauty, victories, and triumphs. No matter what station or class we find ourselves in life, at some point, we will face battles. Whether we are Christians, non-Christians, or even anti-Christians, we will face trials and tribulations. No one is exempt. Even children and adolescents face trials and tribulations unprepared. This is life. What is even more alarming is that no one was asked to be born. We did not get to join a meeting or conference with our parents or God to agree to enter this world. We had no voice or choice in our existence on earth. Not even our parents had the choice in selecting exactly the children they have conceived. Life is filled with unpredictability, uncertainties, surprises, ups and downs, hills and valleys, ebb and flow. God causes "His sun to rise on the evil and the good and sends rain on the righteous and the unrighteous" (Matthew 5:45, NIV). Life isn't fair. Life often doesn't make sense. However, God will make things right in His way and timing. Our duty as children of God is to trust Him in the meantime, no matter what

Introduction

transpires. This is our highest calling—the calling of faith and trust in the face of life's great unknowns!

> " *This is our highest calling—the calling of faith and trust in the face of life's great unknowns!*

The beauty of following Jesus Christ is that we have a guide in this life. This guide is the Holy Spirit, the third person of the Holy Trinity. The Holy Trinity is often misunderstood even to the best theologians the world has seen. There is a great mystery to the Holy Trinity. This mystery should be expected since no human can fully grasp a thrice Holy God. God is one in essence (ontologically) but manifests in three different persons. This is fully displayed when John the Baptist baptized Jesus in the river Jordan (see Matthew 3:13-17). John saw "the Spirit of God [the Holy Spirit] descending like a dove and alighting upon Him. And suddenly a voice came from heaven [God the Father], saying, "This is My beloved Son [Jesus], in whom I am well pleased." The Holy Spirit is a being with a mind, emotions, and will who "searches all things, even the deep things of God" (1 Corinthians 2:10-11). We know the Holy Spirit is a person because the Bible teaches that He thinks and knows (1 Corinthians 2:10), He can be grieved (Ephesians 4:30), and He intercedes for us (Romans 8:26-27). He makes decisions according to His will (1 Corinthians 12:7-11). The Holy Spirit is the Spirit of truth, which illuminates our eyes about spiritual and natural matters. He also functions as our Comforter and Counsellor (John 14:16).

The Holy Spirit was present under the Old Covenant in a limited capacity. However, Jesus promised to send the Holy Spirit to live within believers under the New Covenant brought about by His perfect sacrifice. While the apostles were in the upper room on the Day of Pentecost united on one accord, "suddenly there came a sound from Heaven, as of a rushing mighty wind, and it filled the whole house where they were sitting" (Acts 2:1). The Holy Spirit entered our realm in full capacity and has been executing the function of the Godhead. "They were filled with the Holy Spirit and began speaking in tongues, as the Spirit gave them utterance" (Acts 2:2-4). Upon conversion, the Holy Spirit immediately takes residence in our spirits when we place our faith in Jesus Christ of Nazareth. Can you imagine God's Holy Spirit residing in unholy vessels? This is the mystery and beauty of God. This paradox and others are difficult for human minds to grasp and comprehend. The Holy Spirit empowers us to do the will of God, execute His purposes, and overcome obstacles in our path. He is our power source!

Introduction

> *The Holy Spirit empowers us to do the will of God, execute His purposes, and overcome obstacles in our path. He is our power source!*

My life's journey so far has been very tumultuous yet also a powerful testament to the power of the Holy Spirit and the glory of God. I am a 24-year-old young woman from a rural community in the parish of Manchester, Jamaica. My life was very quiet growing up in the community of Mile Gully. I am considered the baby girl among my six siblings: the little sister. For 19 years of my life, I lived a normal life with no history of mental illness. That would change the day I attended a party with some friends. I was young, naïve, and wanted to fit in with everyone just as anyone else that age would have liked. Little did I know trying to fit in almost cost me my sanity, divine destiny, and life. My youth was almost entirely stripped away from me by evil forces. However, God had another plan: He used the attacks I've experienced to demonstrate His power to deliver me from demonic spirits, heal my wounds, and restore my life and identity.

> *God had another plan: He used the attacks I've experienced to demonstrate His power to deliver me from demonic spirits, heal my wounds, and restore my life and identity.*

This book was inspired by the Holy Spirit to shed light on mental illnesses based on my personal experiences and to shine a brighter light on the power of the Holy Spirit to heal, deliver, and restore identity. Of all the attacks I've experienced, I believe the most significant attack was the one on my identity. Mental illness had caused me to have many embarrassing and humiliating experiences. I felt rejected, unheard, ostracised, vilified—left to accept a fate that my life was permanently ruined. I was made to feel like a "nobody," just an aberration of human existence. I have attempted suicide many times to end my tormented life. I wanted to give up, but God didn't allow me to.

> " I have attempted suicide many times to end my tormented life. I wanted to give up, but God didn't allow me to.

In this book, I explore the scientific perspective of the mind. My goal is for my readers to understand the scientific and medical basics of the mind and mental health as a contextual foundation for grasping my deliverance. Through much of the Middle Ages, science was assigned the status of a "handmaiden to theology." This concept implies that science was not pursued for its own sake but only for the aid it could provide in interpreting the Holy Scripture. Science and nature can help us better understand spiritual truths. I have made many visits to doctors and other healthcare professionals and have been hospitalized

Introduction

on some occasions. I believe God has gifted and equipped healthcare professionals with skills to help people overcome medical problems. However, while medical science has its place, I believe that my deliverance from mental illness was through the power of the Holy Spirit. My deliverance would be called a miracle – an event or phenomenon that cannot be explained by natural or scientific laws and is therefore considered a work of divine agency.

> *Science and nature can help us better understand spiritual truths. While medical science has its place, I believe that my deliverance from mental illness was through the power of the Holy Spirit.*

My exploration of my experience with mental illness and research have highlighted the great need for people struggling with mental illnesses to feel safe to express themselves without fear of discrimination or being labelled as "crazy." The stigma attached to mental illness has caused many to retreat in fear and suffer in silence. People must understand the importance of being active and empathetic listeners to support those struggling with mental illnesses. I strongly believe that mental health education should be a mandatory part of our school curriculum, starting at the basic school level. With that, mental health should be a normalized topic of discussion among family members, friends, social groups, churches, etc. Preschoolers from three to five years old are already taught to identify different emotions. They can recognize happy, surprised, angry, and sad faces and understand each emotion. Identifying and dealing with emotions is necessary to having emotional intelligence. Mental illnesses sometimes develop from traumas that affect an individual from a young age. Sometimes, our negative words or actions, even to preschoolers or infants, can leave a lasting scar on them for a lifetime if not addressed immediately. Creating safe spaces and places for people to express themselves begins at a tender age, mostly in homes and academic institutions. It will be more effective to deal with issues when "small seeds" are planted in the soil before germinating. Digging up these bad seeds and getting rid of them immediately, rather than waiting for them to grow into a strong, rooted tree that bears bad fruits, will help society flourish. Cutting down a fully-grown tree takes a lot of time and energy. With that said, people shouldn't wait until situations get overwhelming and out of control to the point where they are difficult to talk about. We must act now!

Introduction

> *The stigma attached to mental illness has caused many to retreat in fear and suffer in silence.*
> *Creating safe spaces and places for people to express themselves begins at a tender age, mostly in homes and academic institutions.*

Discrimination and stigmatization against those suffering from mental illnesses are two factors that prevent people from seeking and receiving the help, care, and treatment they need on their way to recovery. When persons know someone is battling with a mental health issue, they are automatically labelled with harsh Jamaican terms such as "mad" or "sick head nuh good." Those words are extremely damaging emotionally and mentally. Those persons are written off from society. Society devalues and rejects them, making it difficult for them to gain or keep employment, attend school, or function in their homes. The healing process becomes more difficult when love isn't shown to those persons but instead constant avoidance and ridicule. If more individuals receive family support, love, and constant care like I had, then perhaps the number of suicides would decrease, and maybe some individuals would not experience severe mental conditions. We only exacerbate the problem when we add fuel to a burning fire. One may ask, "Why would God create persons struggling with mental illnesses without divine purposes?" I believe one reason why God allows mental illnesses or physical illnesses is for us to learn the divine virtues of humility, compassion, and patience from dealing with our loved ones or others facing these challenges.

> " If more individuals receive family support, love, and constant care like I had, then perhaps the number of suicides would decrease, and maybe some individuals would not experience severe mental conditions. We only exacerbate the problem when we add fuel to a burning fire.

We may not fully know and understand why God allows these unfortunate life occurrences and conditions; however, we can gain valuable spiritual insights from a passage of scripture where Jesus addressed a question His disciples asked concerning a man born blind. John 9:1-5 records the account of Jesus passing by and seeing a man blind from birth. His disciples asked, "Rabbi [teacher], who sinned, this man or his parents, that he was born blind?" Jesus answered, "Neither this man nor his parents sinned, but God's works should be revealed in him." Notice carefully that this man's blindness was not his or his parent's fault. God allowed this man to be born blind to reveal the works of God in him. God's glory would be revealed when He restored this man's sight, thus demonstrating His marvelous power over blindness. In a turn of events, Jesus "spat on the ground and made clay with the saliva; and He anointed the eyes of the blind

Introduction

man with the clay. And He said to him, 'Go, wash in the pool of Siloam.' So, he went and washed, and came back seeing (verses 6-7).'" Similarly, God allowed me to be attacked by evil forces to reveal His glory through my miraculous deliverance and healing. Through my story, we know that God has the power to deliver from mental illnesses.

Unfortunately, people can be unkind, bitter, and evil at times, allowing the devil to use them to carry out his evil agenda. The Bible brings to our awareness that "we do not wrestle against flesh and blood, but against principalities, against powers, against the rulers of the darkness of this age, against spiritual hosts of wickedness in the heavenly places" (Ephesians 6:12). Sin, the devil, and evil spirits are behind all forms and manner of wickedness. Some individuals allow the spirits of covetousness, hatred, jealousy, and other evil spirits to fill their hearts and consume them. Those spirits serve as open doors for evil to enter and destroy our lives. In Genesis 4:7, Cain was warned that "... sin lies at the door. And its desire is for you, but you should rule over it." Cain had the opportunity to control his anger, but instead, he allowed anger to consume him, which eventually led to him murdering his brother, Abel. Anger, jealousy, and covetousness were open doors that led to the evil act of murder.

> God allowed this man to be born blind to reveal the works of God in him. God's glory would be revealed when He restored this man's sight, thus demonstrating His marvelous power over blindness.

The devil knows God has a purpose for every single individual before we were conceived in our mother's womb. The Word of God states, "Before I formed you in the womb I knew you; Before you were born, I sanctified you; I ordained you a prophet to the nations" (Jeremiah 1:5). Jeremiah, known as the "weeping prophet" wrote, "For I know the thoughts I think toward you, says the Lord, thoughts of peace and not of evil, to give you a future and a hope" (Jeremiah 29:11). We need to internalize this truth that God is for us and not against us. God not only thinks of us; He thinks toward us. That means God thinks in our direction to take us where He wants us to be. His thoughts are for us to arrive at a peaceful place with Him and ourselves. To this point, author John Feinberg wrote, "Jeremiah's words 'hope and a future' are literally 'an end and a hope,' which is a hendiadys (a figure in which a complex idea is expressed in two words linked by a coordinating conjunction) and means 'a hopeful end.'" Even when we suffer, God has a future and hope for us. The devil wants to deceive and rob us of our sense of God's future and hope for us. Suffering from mental illnesses or any other form of illnesses does not mean

Introduction

God doesn't have a future and hope for us. God can use that suffering as the catalyst to give us a purposeful life and to lead many broken souls to Him. Jesus Christ came not just to give us life, but to give us abundant life, a life that is satisfied and contented in Him despite the vicissitudes of life (see John 10:10). Theologian James Montgomery Boice wrote, "The Greek word for abundance, 'perissos,' has a mathematical meaning and generally denotes a surplus…The abundant life is above all the contented life, in which our contentment is based upon the fact that God is equal to every emergency and can supply all our needs according to His riches and glory in Christ Jesus.'"

> " Even when we suffer, God has a future and hope for us. Suffering from mental illnesses or any other form of illnesses does not mean God doesn't have a future and hope for us. God can use that suffering as the catalyst to give us a purposeful life and to lead many broken souls to Him.

As believers in Christ, even when we face mental illnesses, we firmly believe that we have an abundant life because our hope is in Jesus, the Hope of Glory. The enemy tried to use the device of witchcraft to alter or destroy my divine purpose and destiny. The power of darkness is real, but the power of light demonstrated through the Holy Spirit is greater to dismantle all powers of darkness. A higher power always puts a lower power in check, implying supremacy of the higher power. The forces of darkness were vehemently against me with the goal for me to lose full consciousness of my mind and/or commit suicide. The enemy targeted my mind to have me under his control because where the mind goes, the person follows.

> "The power of darkness is real, but the power of light demonstrated through the Holy Spirit is greater to dismantle all powers of darkness. A higher power always puts a lower power in check, implying supremacy of the higher power.

Beloved, is there anything too hard for the Lord? I fervently believe that there is nothing too hard for Him. Beloved, whose report shall I believe? I will believe the report of the Lord Jesus Christ of Nazareth. I reject all other reports. God's power is absolute, limitless, and boundless. He is an eternal God who reserves the right to step into time at any given moment and set in motion that which serves His sovereign will. Just by placing unwavering faith in Him, even a broken mind like the state mine was in can be delivered, healed, and restored by the power of the Holy Spirit from demonic strongholds and powers. Today, I can boldly declare through the power of the Holy Spirit, "I have a sound mind in Christ Jesus. I identify with Christ Jesus."

Introduction

> **❝** *Beloved, whose report shall I believe? I will believe the report of the Lord Jesus Christ of Nazareth. I reject all other reports.*

God has also predestined us. The God of this vast, incomprehensible universe has given us our destinies before the foundations of the world. Paul writes in Romans 8:29-30, "For those God foreknew he also predestined to be conformed to the image of his Son, that he might be the firstborn among many brothers and sisters. And those he predestined, he also called; those he called, he also justified; those he justified, he also glorified." This is referred to as the doctrine of election. God knew us before we were born. He foreknew us; He predestined us to conform to Jesus' image; He called us; He justified us; He will glorify us. What an amazing God we serve! Paul also writes, "He predestined us for adoption to sonship through Jesus Christ, in accordance with His pleasure and will" (Ephesians 1:5). Our role is to have faith in Jesus and allow the Holy Spirit to lead us on the path He has set before us. We were adopted into the family of God by the perfect sacrifice of Jesus Christ. Each child of God has been given a God-given purpose and destiny. This is what Satan wants to steal from us through evil mediums such as witchcraft. However, we were given free will—the ability to choose. By submitting our will to the will of God, we allow the Holy Spirit to help and empower us to do what pleases Him. "For it is God who works in you both to will and to do for His good pleasure" (Philippians 2:13). When our will is aligned with God's will, we start to walk in God's plan, purpose, will, and destiny for our lives.

> *By submitting our will to the will of God, we allow the Holy Spirit to help and empower us to do what pleases Him.*

Let us begin the journey...

"When you completely trust a person, you'll get one of two results: a friend for a life or a lesson for a life."

— Unknown

Chapter 1

Early Life

Please allow me to properly introduce myself. My name is Shannese Davidson. I was born in 1999 in the rural area of Mile Gully District in the cool parish of Manchester. I am the sixth child of my parents, Audrey Davidson and Ashley Davidson. They conceived seven children, blessing me with three brothers and three sisters. Both parents raised me—my mother worked as a domestic helper, and my father as a farmer. I'm not from a wealthy background, but my mother went above and beyond through hard work and sacrifice to ensure that our daily needs were met and that we weren't deprived of a good education.

I started my early education at Mile Gully Basic School. After completing my early childhood education, I transitioned to Mile Gully Primary. Since I lived near the school, I was able to commute by foot. In the fifth grade, my mother decided to transfer me to Top Hill All Age and Infant School because she

Early Life

recognized I wasn't performing to my fullest potential. Mrs. Williams, the principal at the time who lived in my district, brought me to and from school to reduce the financial struggles of paying taxi fares. She also assisted me academically by ensuring I stayed back for extra classes and studied as I waited for her in the mornings or after school. After I sat and passed the Grade Six Achievement Test (GSAT), I successfully transitioned to May Day High School.

While growing up, I was more of an introvert; I was soft-spoken and extremely shy. During my adolescent years, I struggled mainly with social changes. Due to my personality, it was difficult for me to adjust to different environments. I struggled to make friends. Public speaking and presentations at school were also challenging for me. Introducing myself as I transitioned to different schools or within different classes was like a nightmare. I disliked it when so much attention was focused on me just for an introduction. Self-esteem was not an issue; I just preferred being unnoticed. As I changed environments by attending May Day High, I came out of my shell a little and began making friends.

Reflecting on my early life, I recognized that, like my mother, I was passionate about helping others and cleaning. I remember doing simple things like attending school early, sometimes in the mornings, at Mile Gully Primary School to sweep the school compound. When I transitioned to Top Hill All Age and Infant School, I excitedly assisted the janitor by cleaning classrooms. I also helped wash dishes in the canteens of both primary schools after the students had lunch. It was a joy for me to help lessen the workload for others.

When I started having close friends, I recognized God placed a compassionate heart within me toward others and a willingness to give. According to Acts 20:35, "I have shown you in every way, by laboring like this, that you must support the weak. And remember the words of the Lord Jesus, that He said, 'It is more blessed to give than to receive.'" Although I was not yet a Christian, I was blessed with a giving heart. The earliest point in life I can remember such an act of kindness was at primary school. My mom provided me with enough funds to get something to eat for my break because I collected lunch from the path program. Instead of getting something for myself, I bought something for my grade five teacher for her to eat during this period. It wasn't because she was in need, or I wanted to be the teacher's pet; it was the way I knew how to express love and appreciation towards her. I didn't know how to express myself by speaking it verbally; I knew how to act or write it.

Early Life

> *It was a joy for me to help lessen the workload for others. I didn't know how to express myself by speaking it verbally; I knew how to act or write it.*

Within the same grade, I saw one of my classmates who was in need. Despite my family's financial struggle, I went home and requested my mother to buy a 'ballet' pair of shoes for her. At the time, it was common and affordable in the Jamaican stores. Out of the little she had, my mother purchased the pair of shoes for me to present to this individual, and although it wasn't much, it was indeed a joy to place a smile on my classmate's face. The act of giving was the principle that guided my life.

Giving out of having little was something my mother instilled within me. Although I wanted to give, I learned the sacrificial way because I had very little. When I attended high school, a few times some of my friends would reach out to inform me that they couldn't attend school on a particular day. Out of consideration, I investigated the reason and learned that it was due to financial issues. Although I wasn't given any extra funds that day, I divided the money I received. I subtracted my taxi fare and gave the rest to the individual, just enough to pay their fare. We then collected lunch from the path program. As I grew older, whenever I saw something in my family's possession that I believed someone I came across was more in need of, I would request it be given to the person. Whenever I ask my family members about things someone could benefit from, they asked, "Who do you want it to give to now?"

> As I grew older, whenever I saw something in my family's possession that I believed someone I came across was more in need of, I would request it be given to the person.

Friends came into my life during my tenure in high school, while some left. I wasn't bothered by this, for I understood some individuals are placed in our lives for a season, while few are for a lifetime. I had a small friendship circle at the end of fourth form at May Day High School. We thought such a friendship would last forever. I tried my best to keep the friendship going. I ensured no one was sad around me. I would find the simplest things to make them laugh. Sometimes, I could hardly express myself to them because I was already laughing at my jokes. That would make them laugh even more. We spent much time together, hanging out on weekends or free sessions at school, studying, talking, and laughing. We tried to balance our academic and social lives. However, we weren't the ones to go to parties or were among the popular groups at school. That didn't bother us because we wanted to enjoy every moment spent together. Little did I know that the beginning of such a beautiful friendship would lead to an unexpected end.

Early Life

> ❝ I understood some individuals are placed in our lives for a season, while few are for a lifetime.
> Little did I know that the beginning of such a beautiful friendship would lead to an unexpected end.

Shannese in 2nd form and graduating from May Day High School.

A Sound Mind

Shannese successfully graduated from Top Hill All Age & Infant School in 2012. Supported by family, former principal, Mrs. Williams, and former teacher, Mr Henry.

Early Life

Shannese at ages 17 and 18.

A Sound Mind

Family photo of Shannese and her family supporting her sister's graduation.

"But difficult situations and wrong choices conspire to trap us in hopelessness."

— Judah Smith

Chapter 2

A Prey In The Enemy's Trap

Prey is the weakest animal in the animal kingdom, while the predator is deemed to be the strongest. For instance, a lion is classified as a predator to a zebra. A zebra is classified as prey simply because a lion has enough power to capture and kill the zebra. A snake is classified as a predator to a mouse. A mouse is prey simply because it cannot kill the snake when it attacks—the snake would overpower and consume the mouse. To be preyed upon is to be regarded as weak and inferior to predators. Predators tend to target the most vulnerable ones and exploit areas of weakness.

> *To be preyed upon is to be regarded as weak and inferior to predators. Predators tend to target the most vulnerable ones and exploit areas of weakness.*
> *The enemy will use family or friends ignorantly or knowingly to assist in ambushing God's children.*

The people of God were referred to as prey as mentioned in Isaiah 49:24: "Shall the prey be taken from the mighty, or the lawful captive delivered?" As God's children, we are viewed as prey to the enemy of our souls. The enemy is portrayed in Scripture as a roaring lion, seeking whom he may devour (1 Peter 5:8). As a result, we are admonished to "be sober and vigilant" because our adversary is intentionally looking to destroy us and God's purposes for our lives. In the animal kingdom, a lion is known as a predator. Likewise, Satan is metaphorically referred to as a lion with the nature of a predator to devour—consuming purposes, destinies, and even lives. Satan is portrayed as ferocious, ruthless, powerfully aggressive, bent on defending its turf, and often working to ambush God's children. The enemy will use family or friends ignorantly or knowingly to assist in ambushing God's children. However, we can take comfort in knowing God will deliver us from the traps or plots of the enemy, as indicated in Isaiah 24:25: "...the prey of the terrible shall be delivered: for I [God] will contend with him who contends with you, and I [God] will save your children." We have a God who fights for His children and will deliver us from all predators.

A Sound Mind

> As God's children, we are viewed as prey to the enemy of our souls. Satan is metaphorically referred to as a lion with the nature of a predator to devour—consuming purposes, destinies, and even lives.
>
> We have a God who fights for His children and will deliver us from all predators.

Humanity was created to dominate the entire earth and its inhabitants. In Genesis 1:26-30, God gave man dominion over every beast of the earth, fowl of the air, and everything that creeps upon the earth. After humanity's fall in the Garden of Eden, Satan had the opportunity to take dominion over humanity and all human affairs. (Genesis 3:14). Unfortunately, humanity forfeited dominion to Satan by succumbing to his deceitful tricks. By placing our faith in the perfect sacrifice of Jesus Christ, we regain our authority over the enemy. However, we must understand this authority and walk in it. In Genesis 3:15, God pronounced judgment over Satan: "I will put enmity between you and the woman and between your seed and her seed; he shall bruise your head, and you shall bruise his heel." This important verse is referred to as "the protoevangelium," the first gospel where God pronounced judgment on Satan. Jesus Christ won the ultimate victory at Calvary's Cross to redeem humanity. Accordingly, we do not have to live as prey or fear predators. We can live a life of victory by walking and living in the victory of

Jesus Christ. As Christians, we live and operate from a posture of a victory already won. Our warfare is a fixed one.

> ❝ Jesus Christ won the ultimate victory at Calvary's Cross to redeem humanity. Accordingly, we do not have to live as prey or fear predators. We can live a life of victory by walking and living in the victory of Jesus Christ.
> As Christians, we live and operate from a posture of a victory already won. Our warfare is a fixed one.

The body of Christ, through the Holy Spirit, has the power to overcome and defeat the predator, Satan, and his demonic kingdom. In the Old Testament, the Holy Spirit did not indwell God's people, but He came upon them and gave them the power to achieve things they would not have accomplished on their own. The story of Saul is an example. When Saul was anointed king of Israel, the Holy Spirit came upon him (1 Samuel 10:10), but when God removed His blessing from Saul, the Holy Spirit left him (1 Samuel 16:14). Before Jesus ascended into Heaven, He promised that He would officially send the Holy Spirit, and this time He will abide in us forever (John 14:16-26).

> ❝ By placing our faith in the perfect sacrifice of Jesus Christ, we regain our authority over the enemy. However, we must understand this authority and walk in it.

On the Day of Pentecost, the Holy Spirit descended upon all believers of Christ, marking the Church's birth. (Acts 2:1-4) Today, the Church has the power of the Holy Spirit to defeat predators by trampling on serpents and scorpions, and over all the power of the enemy: and nothing shall hurt us by any means (Luke 10:19). Jesus has given His followers power and authority to trample on serpents and scorpions. Today, we can demonstrate such power and authority through the Holy Spirit, knowing that nothing shall by any means hurt us.

> *Jesus has given His followers power and authority to trample on serpents and scorpions. Today, we can demonstrate such power and authority through the Holy Spirit, knowing that nothing shall by any means hurt us.*

According to I John 4:4, "You are of God, little children, and have overcome them because He who is in you is greater than he who is in the world." We are confident knowing that we have supernatural power to overcome the predator, Satan, through the Holy Spirit who dwells in us. The One who is greater than any force in the world, mighty in battle and a man of war, is fighting for us. Therefore, we can stand firm, knowing that He is the ultimate Overcomer, and so we have overcome. 2 Chronicles 20:15 states, "... the battle is not yours, but God's."

All that is required of us is to place our faith in God, obey His instructions, and allow Him to do the rest.

> " We are confident knowing that we have supernatural power to overcome the predator, Satan, through the Holy Spirit who dwells in us. The One who is greater than any force in the world, mighty in battle and a man of war, is fighting for us.

A Trap Set by the Enemy

My friends and I successfully graduated from May Day High School. As we moved on to the next phase of our lives, planning to further our studies or enter the working world, we tried to figure things out as we stayed motivated and focused. We were ready to conquer all the challenges ahead of us. Maintaining our friendship was one of the challenges we didn't know we would have encountered. A few of us grew apart, and for some, we encountered situations where we decided to walk away from each other without any acrimony or controversy—however, the three of us who remained stood together as we overcame challenges and changes. We always found a way to work out our differences and stick together. We became more than friends; we were like sisters.

We went to different schools, furthering our education as we followed our respective career paths. Yet, we still made time to spend together. We met after classes or a few Saturdays to grab something to eat at "Juici Patties" restaurant or the Mandeville food court. Sometimes, we met at Grove Court to socialize. We found the latter more effective than just texting and talking. We went to several places together like the river or had sleepovers. People tend to prioritize work or school while forgetting loved ones and friends, but that was never an issue among us. Constant communication and spending quality time together were very important to us.

On Saturday, September 8, 2018, I celebrated my 19th birthday. As the day drew closer, I was excited to celebrate it with my friends. We had conversations about it, but we never finalized any plans. All we knew was it was a must for us to go out. I gathered funds from my family and went to Mandeville a few days in advance to purchase the perfect outfit for that day. I thought white looked outstanding on special events, so I wanted a white outfit. When I finally saw a white Adidas crop top blouse with a white matching high-waist skirt, I knew that was the outfit I wanted. I happily purchased it. My friends and I discussed the hairstyle I wanted to get done. As we discussed, I considered getting a long braid to my waist length. My motive was to go all out, looking attractive and extraordinary. They didn't discuss much about themselves since it would be my special day. The focus was on me for that period. However, my main desire was to celebrate my birthday with them.

The day before my birthday, I bought several packs of braids in Mandeville, including black and burgundy braids. I then came to my home district, Mile Gully, seeking a hairdresser to get my hair done. To my disappointment, a few hairdressers said they couldn't have done my hair because it was too short. Thankfully, I found a person who decided to take up the task. She started my hair that same day but could not finish it because it was late, so I went home to return early the next morning. I woke up excited the following morning because it was finally my birthday. I woke up to numerous text messages from family and friends, which kept coming in throughout the day. It added to my excitement and made me feel extremely loved and special. My mother and siblings sang the happy birthday song, and everyone around me was so excited that I turned nineteen. I rushed to the bathroom, brushed my teeth, washed my face, and bathed. After that, I had breakfast and hurried to the hairdresser's house to finish my hair. When my hair was finished, a lot of time passed, but I was pleased with how it turned out, especially because people complimented me as I made my way back home.

My friends and I still hadn't decided where to go, but it didn't matter once I had the opportunity to spend the day with them. I finally arrived home. It seemed like it would rain, so my family tried to convince me to stay home, but I was too excited and determined to celebrate my birthday. I called my friends, and we agreed on a time to meet. I then got dressed. I was so excited to put on my new outfit. I asked my sister, Shanniel, to do my makeup. After completing it, I put on a few pieces of jewelry – a foot anklet and a chain. Shanniel took a few pictures of me while she gave compliments, making me feel good. Thankfully, my family had gifted me with funds to enjoy myself before I headed out. When my friends and I met, it was about 5 pm. We idled a little while we waited for individuals to leave work or arrive in Mandeville, as my friends invited other individuals. When we gathered, we ate enough cooked food to sustain our stomachs. Our motive was to try something new. I wanted to experience drinking alcoholic beverages for the first time. As we laughed, talked, and walked in Mandeville, we headed for the final stop at a bar as it was getting late.

> *Life has a way of presenting unexpected twists and turns.*

Life has a way of presenting unexpected twists and turns. One minute, you're having a fantastic time with your friends celebrating your birthday, then the next minute, you're asking

A Prey In The Enemy's Trap

God how I got into this predicament. When one isn't sober or vigilant, just enjoying the "moment" in a sensual, fleshy way, one gets caught in the devil's trap, which comes unexpectedly or suddenly upon us. Little did I know, I was walking directly into the enemy's trap. Ignorantly, I was like prey, as the fishes taken in the snare of the devil's evil net or as the birds caught in the snare (see Ecclesiastes 9:12).

> *One minute, you're having a fantastic time with your friends celebrating your birthday, then the next minute, you're asking God how I got into this predicament. When one isn't sober or vigilant, just enjoying the "moment" in a sensual, fleshy way, one gets caught in the devil's trap, which comes unexpectedly or suddenly upon us.*

A Sound Mind

Photo taken of Shannese on September 8, 2019 before leaving home to celebrate her 19th Birthday.

> "Your history does not need to define your destiny."
>
> — Christine Caine

Chapter 3

Birthday Gone Wrong

Birthdays are special events that most individuals look forward to annually. This is a celebration of our existence, where we usually gather with loved ones and friends to create lasting memories. It is a day filled with laughter, joy, happiness, and fun. Some individuals tend to start planning months in advance for this special day—what to wear, where to celebrate, and with whom. They would also expect to receive gifts or surprises on this special occasion. We don't expect birthdays to be "bad days." As far as I can remember, my birthdays normally fall on school days. The most I would do was eat something special on that day, order something different from the school menu, or go to Kentucky Fried Chicken (KFC) in Mandeville after school to eat. However, on my 19th birthday, I decided to do something different—dress up, go out, eat, drink, and take lots of pictures.

In the evening, my friends and I went to a bar in Mandeville for my birthday. They started ordering what they wanted—mixing

Birthday Gone Wrong

juices with liquor. They asked me what I wanted, and within the same minute, my friend's co-worker offered to pay for anything I requested since it was my special day. At that moment, I thought it was okay to get drunk, something I saw regularly. I thought, "People had fun going out and getting drunk, and then the next day, they were okay, right?" I told the bartender I wanted nineteen shots of white rum, signifying my nineteenth birthday, with no water added. I knew nothing about drinking; I just wanted to experience it. The bartender asked if I was sure that was what I wanted, so I asked my friends what they thought. One of my friends asked if I was sure, and the other said I should go ahead once that's what I wanted. So, I told the bartender to proceed with my request.

> " I thought, "People had fun going out and getting drunk, and then the next day, they were okay, right?" I told the bartender I wanted nineteen shots of white rum, signifying my nineteenth birthday, with no water added.

After taking my first shot, I realized it was the most unpleasant thing I've ever tasted, so I thought probably it wasn't drinking alcoholic beverages that people enjoyed but the after-effect. I took another shot and felt a bit tipsy, slightly drunk. My former friend and her partner at the time, along with others, were boosting me up. In Jamaican culture, with a little "hype," we tend to try to prove a point. After I drank the two shots, my former friend said I should walk in a straight line back and forth in the bar three times before I continued. I did that, and I was perfectly fine, but then she gave me some liquid in a cup that she was drinking and told me to drink it. She strongly insisted that for me to continue with the shots, I had to drink what was in the cup that she gave me. Without thinking that through, I drank what was in the cup.

> " I did that, and I was perfectly fine, but then she gave me some liquid in a cup that she was drinking and told me to drink it. She strongly insisted that for me to continue with the shots, I had to drink what was in the cup that she gave me. Without thinking that through, I drank what was in the cup.

Afterwards, I took a third shot of rum. I felt disoriented and lost consciousness. I remembered regaining consciousness and noticing her other friends who had come along that weren't there before. They laughed and made fun of me while helping me as I staggered into their vehicle to go to Bank House Mall in Mandeville. I was in and out of consciousness, but I remembered when we arrived at Bank House Mall. They were discussing what to do since I was so drunk. I remembered telling my former friend I didn't want to go home. I refused to allow my family to see me in such a condition that I'd never been in before. I begged her to allow me to stay at her place until the morning when I got sober; then, I would go home.

At some point, I recalled being emotional while looking at my former friend. I felt confused and called her another person's name. I told her how much I hated her and how she was the reason for all that had transpired. I told her she should have stopped me when she saw I was going too far. When I became sober and remembered the things I said, I was deeply sorry for my unkind words. Individuals believe that when one is drunk, they tend to speak exactly how they feel. In my case, I didn't hate her and shouldn't have blamed her because it was something I wanted to experience for myself. I deeply regretted my choice because of the unforgettable bad experience. However, I wondered why she strongly insisted that I drank what was in the cup she gave me, and the content of the substance I drank. After that chaotic night, my former friend's partner drove us to her home so I could sleep for the night. A birthday that started so well ended up in catastrophe. Little did I know, this was the inception of a severe spiritual warfare that almost took my life.

> *A birthday that started so well ended up in catastrophe. Little did I know, this was the inception of a severe spiritual warfare that almost took my life.*

"I'm most afraid of losing my mind. You lose your identity, sense of who you are, where you are."

— STEPHEN KING

Chapter 4

Hospital Visitation

There is an old saying, "dead men tell no tales." This is an idiom used to say that someone who has been killed cannot reveal secret information or reveal the truth about the cause of their death. For instance, we will never understand what a person who commits suicide has seriously been through unless they left behind a suicidal note—their last words of hopelessness. We will never understand that person's brokenness or depressive, hurt feelings to the point that they lost their voice. For some people struggling with mental illnesses, it is so severe that they, too, have lost their voice to express their emotions. When a person loses their voice, their story can be told in millions of different ways by many different people until the story eventually fades away. Noone can tell your story better than you do. Don't allow mental illness to stop you from telling your story.

Hospital Visitation

> *When a person loses their voice, their story can be told in millions of different ways by many different people until the story eventually fades away.*
> *Noone can tell your story better than you do. Don't allow mental illness to stop you from telling your story.*

The Mayo Clinic Staff defined mental illness, also called mental health disorders, as a wide range of mental health conditions — disorders that affect your mood, thinking, and behavior. Examples of mental illnesses include depression, anxiety disorders, schizophrenia, eating disorders, and addictive behaviors. Many people have mental health concerns from time to time. However, a mental health concern becomes a mental illness when ongoing signs and symptoms cause frequent stress and affect your ability to function. Mental illness is nothing to be ashamed of. Like heart disease or diabetes, mental illness is also a medical problem that can be corrected and managed. Psychiatrists are medical doctors who have completed specialized training to diagnose, treat, and address mental, emotional, and behavioral disorders. Where necessary, psychiatrists prescribe psychotropic medications to correct and manage biochemical imbalances in the brain or otherwise to relieve depression, anxiety, and other painful emotional states.

A Sound Mind

> ❝ Mental illness is nothing to be ashamed of. Like heart disease or diabetes, mental illness is also a medical problem that can be corrected and managed.

Since the fall of humanity, people have struggled with mental illnesses. The Bible shows examples of men and women of God who exhibited symptoms of depression, anxiety, and other types of mental illnesses. Martha, David, and Jeremiah are a few examples. Overwhelmed by the demands as hostess, Martha grew angry toward her sister, who sat at the feet of Christ instead of helping to prepare a meal for the guests. Frustrated, Martha finally approached Jesus and said, "Lord, do you not care that my sister left me to do all the work alone? Tell her to come and help me." The Lord Jesus answered her, "Martha, Martha, you are anxious and upset about many things when only one thing is necessary" (Luke 10:40-42 NCB). Through Jesus' response, Martha gained understanding and recognized that there was no need to be anxious. According to Philippians 4:6-7, "Be anxious for nothing, but in everything by prayer and supplication, with thanksgiving, let your requests be made known to God; and the peace of God, which surpasses all understanding, will guard your hearts and minds through Christ Jesus." The prophet Jeremiah often referred to us as "weeping prophet" struggled with depression and loneliness. In Jeremiah 20: 14-18, he lamented about his existence:

Hospital Visitation

> "Cursed be the day in which I was born! Let the day not be blessed in which my mother bore me! Let the man curse who brought news to my father, saying, "A male child has been born to you!" Making him very glad. And let that man be like the cities which the LORD overthrew and did not relent; Let him hear the cry in the morning and the shouting at noon, because he did not kill me from the womb, that my mother might have been my grave, and her womb always enlarged with me. Why did I come forth from the womb to see labor and sorrow, that my days should be consumed with shame?"

Although God chose Jeremiah from birth to be a prophet to the nation of Judah (Jeremiah 1:4-50), he faced times when he was so distraught about his life and purpose. His question to God in his state of depression was, "Why did I come forth from the womb to see labor and sorrow, that my days should be consumed with shame?" God's response to Jeremiah was a message of hope, assuring the prophet that he would not be alone. He also reminded Jeremiah of the grace He has afforded to him from the start (Jeremiah 15:20-21).

> David, a man after God's own heart, was treated as the least among his brothers. He encountered threats by the king to whom he'd been loyal, and then he was betrayed by his own son, Absalom. David recorded many songs of

lament that reflected his pain and depression, including Psalm 6:6-7 (NIV), "I am worn out from my groaning. All night long I flood my bed with weeping and drench my couch with tears. My eyes grow weak with sorrow; they fail because of all my foes." (Tammy Kensington, June 9, 2023). David recognized how depressed he was and encouraged his soul to hope in God and to put on the garments of praise to overcome (Isaiah 61:3). He stated in Psalms 43:5, "Why are you cast down, O my soul? And why are you disquieted within me? Hope in God; For I shall praise Him, The help of my countenance and my God."

On September 9, 2019, I woke up at my former friend's home. I got up and headed straight to the bathroom to vomit, then went back to the bedroom. I remembered going outside and talking to her about what happened the previous day. She told me how much I vomited throughout the night, but I didn't recall that. I asked her the whereabouts of my missing shoe. She told me many things happened that night, so she didn't know when the shoe went missing. I recognized that I started to feel weak, after which I collapsed, but I didn't lose consciousness. After I regained my balance and felt better, I was ready to go home. I ate breakfast and bought a pair of slippers in the district

Hospital Visitation

to wear on my way home. She followed me to Mandeville since her boyfriend would also be there.

When we arrived in Mandeville, we went to the food court to sit down for a little while because I felt weak. When we were ready to leave, I fainted again. I told her I still wasn't feeling well, so it wouldn't make sense for me to go home. It would be better for me to go to the hospital. A kind stranger approached me when I fainted and decided to help me to get to the hospital, so we went with him. When we arrived at the hospital, I fainted again but also started experiencing on-and-off panic attacks. According to the National Institute of Mental Health, panic disorder is an anxiety disorder characterized by unexpected and repeated episodes of intense fear accompanied by physical symptoms that may include chest pain, heart palpitations, shortness of breath, dizziness, or abdominal distress. These episodes occur "out of the blue," not in conjunction with a known fear or stressor.

They rushed me to the Accident and Emergency department in a wheelchair. A Registered nurse checked my vitals, asked my former friend to register me, and told us to wait for the doctor. Due to my constant panic attacks and fainting episodes, I saw a doctor quickly. I explained what I had done the previous day and how I felt. They asked me questions like what day it was, whether anyone in my family struggled with mental illness, and how I was feeling, along with other questions. I was told I was going to be admitted, so I started to break down in tears, especially when they told me they were going to admit me to the psychiatric ward for schizoaffective disorder. I didn't clearly understand why. After the doctors left and my former friend stood there waiting for the doctor to admit me, she told me everything was going to be alright, then she laughed, saying, "you're officially a psychiatric patient." I was so confused by everything that took place. I finally decided to call my mother and explain what was happening. My former friend's boyfriend showed up and had my missing shoe. Gladly, I asked her where the other shoe was, and she told me she didn't know, although we had it with us when we got to Mandeville.

I was comforted by my mother when she arrived. She provided support and comfort. My siblings and my mother went back and forth, visiting me at the hospital, ensuring I was okay and met all my needs in terms of clothing, sheets, pillow, etc, as well as the foods I requested. The hospital staff informed mom they were admitting me for schizoaffective disorder. Schizoaffective disorder is a mental health disorder that is marked by a combination of schizophrenia symptoms, such as hallucinations or delusions, and mood disorder symptoms, such as depression or mania. Panic attacks and panic disorders are common in patients with schizoaffective disorder (Mayo Staff Clinic, 2019).

Hospital Visitation

Hallucination, delusion, and depression were symptoms I experienced. Hallucination is hearing, seeing, or feeling things that aren't there while being delusional is believing things that aren't true. As I remembered someone in the past who committed suicide by hanging herself, I started to hallucinate, especially when I wore a chain around my neck. I felt the deceased person pulling the chain on my neck, and I cried out for help. I felt delusional, believing this deceased person wanted me to meet at a specific location, so I became fearful whenever I had to pass this location, which I had to pass daily.

Depression appeared to me as a person. I could feel depression physically, and when depression showed up, it demanded attention. I submitted myself to depression and did anything to please it. I searched for depressing movies and watched them, listened to depressing songs, and searched for depressing quotes. I created the atmosphere to accommodate depression, which made me feel extremely weak. When depression had its way with me, it welcomed the spirit of suicide.

> *Depression appeared to me as a person. I could feel depression physically, and when depression showed up, it demanded attention. I submitted myself to depression and did anything to please it.*
>
> *When depression had its way with me, it welcomed the spirit of suicide.*

In the multiple awards-winning movie, "A Beautiful Mind," the character John Nash, played by actor Russel Crowe, is a mathematician who battles with schizophrenia and finds a way to overcome it. John Nash expressed about his hallucinated thoughts, "I've gotten used to ignoring them, and I think, as a result, they've given up on me. I think that's what it's like with all our dreams and our nightmares, Martin; we've got to keep feeding them for them to stay alive." He was referring to the voices and hallucinations which he experienced. Similarly, I experienced this with depression; I kept on giving depression what it needed, and that kept it around. I constantly fed depression. Happiness was a trigger for me—enjoying quality time with friends and family was not accepted in my condition. Depression led me to isolate myself where it could have me do whatever it pleases. Funerals were also a major trigger for me; the atmosphere and being around mournful persons excited my depression the most. When I saw graves, I would walk towards them, attempting to lie down. I heard thoughts in my mind saying, "you are home." The thought would consume my mind, and then I fainted. I also lost my appetite now and then and constantly slept. Because of those symptoms, after I was discharged from the hospital, I was placed in the mental health clinic. I visited monthly to see a psychiatrist and received appointments to receive counselling from a psychologist.

Hospital Visitation

Schizoaffective Disorder is a biological disorder that likely results from an imbalance in brain chemicals. Medical results such as a CT (Computed Tomography) scan and MRI (Magnetic Resonance Imaging) showed non-biochemical imbalances in my brain. However, due to the frequent panic attacks, regular visits to the hospital, and admissions, they kept on increasing the medications. In the hospital, I felt overwhelmed as I saw other mental health patients being restrained, moving in slow motion, constantly sleeping, asking when they could go home, and having outbursts. It was even more heartbreaking when I overheard nurses talking about individuals whose families had left patients and never returned, and they sought places to put them.

My family was my greatest support. I reached out to those I considered my close friends and begged them to visit me. I had to ask my mother to give my former friend taxi fare to visit me so she wouldn't have any excuse not to. My other friend from high school was working, so I guess she didn't have much time to visit, but she did when she could. In such situations, one craves support, care, and love than the norm. When I was finally discharged from the hospital after my first admission, I asked my former friend to stay with me at my home, and she came. I was so grateful for the support I thought I was receiving from her. We even decided to attend church together. At a particular fasting service we attended, we sat down together, and a church sister who was leading the service said, "Some of you, your best friend is going to become your enemy." We looked at each other and laughed. Then we agreed that would never happen to us.

Since both of us were home and mom had to go to work, she asked me to babysit my nephew, who was a few months old. His parents were overseas. Somehow, I felt overwhelmed and frustrated. The constant crying of the baby and wanting to do household chores felt stressful for me. I started to hear negative thoughts, and I entertained them. Through my frustration from not receiving help from my former friend, I laughed and told my nephew I didn't care if he fell off the bed. I laughed as he got closer to the edge. When I came around and recognized what I was about to allow to have happened, I picked up my nephew and put him further on the bed. I left the room in tears upon recognizing my thoughts and actions. Thoughts flustered my mind to end my life, so I went to the kitchen. I started to break down in tears as I tried to fight to overcome the voices I was hearing. I fell on the floor with a knife in my hand. Family members came and brought me back to the hospital. I was admitted yet again.

> When I came around and recognized what I was about to allow to have happened, I picked up my nephew and put

Hospital Visitation

> him further on the bed. I left the room in tears upon recognizing my thoughts and actions. Thoughts flustered my mind to end my life, so I went to the kitchen. I started to break down in tears as I tried to fight to overcome the voices I was hearing. I fell on the floor with a knife in my hand.

During a one-year period, I was in and out of the hospital. The panic attacks and fainting episodes were constant, but I still tried living a normal life as if I wasn't experiencing those things. I felt hurt when I noticed people were embarrassed by the things I was going through. I hated it when people began to pity me when they were aware of my situation. I didn't believe anyone understood what I was going through, so I got tired of explaining over time. They couldn't relate to my situation, I thought; no matter how qualified they were in psychiatric or psychology, they didn't understand what it was like to be in that exact situation. I believed pitying me only encouraged the situation, making me think it was okay. I didn't want to remain in that situation; my main motive was to overcome the condition I felt was holding me back.

> " I believed pitying me only encouraged the situation, making me think it was okay. I didn't want to remain in that situation; my main motive was to overcome the condition I felt was holding me back.

I started listening and entertaining negative thoughts until it got to a point where I got seriously suicidal. There were a few attempts to jump out of moving vehicles and walk in the road when a vehicle approached me. The most serious attempt I made that almost succeeded was after writing a suicidal letter addressed to my loved ones; I then overdosed on the tablets they told me to take for the illness. I broke down in tears, called Mommy, and told her what I did. She rushed home from work and chartered a taxi to take me to the hospital. On my journey there, I was in and out of consciousness. Whenever I came around, I told Mommy I wouldn't make it as I thought my suicidal attempt would have been successful and I would die. The next thing I remembered was being in a hospital. The doctors asked me questions, but they didn't understand my responses. I remembered the doctor telling me to stay awake; then she told me she was putting a tube through my nose to my stomach. She then instructed me that each time she pushed the tube, I should swallow. This is referred to as "nasogastric tube." According to Cleveland Clinic (2022), A nasogastric tube is a type of medical catheter that's inserted through your nose into your stomach. It's used for limited periods to deliver substances such as food or medications to your stomach or to draw substances out. They can also suction out stomach contents to relieve pressure or remove poisons (Cleveland Clinic, 2022). When I became

Hospital Visitation

fully conscious, I saw an extreme dark substance in the drainage bag connected to the nasogastric tube, where it successfully suctioned out the medications I overdosed on.

I had a friend who called me and said, "Shan, you don't have a mental illness." She said it was superstitious, referring to a spiritual attack. I explained to her my entire experience leading up to being diagnosed with a mental disorder. My friend asked me what my former friend had placed in my drink and what she had done with my missing shoe. I constantly asked my former friend about the contents of my drink, but she kept telling me she placed nothing in the drink. My friend and her family, who didn't believe I had a mental illness, took me to their home to stay. I also thought I needed a change of environment. They showered me with genuine love and care. They brought me to churches, trying to get a breakthrough. My mother followed me to some churches. However, I couldn't stay in churches—I felt extremely uncomfortable, so I walked out, started to have panic attacks, fainted, or said things that disturbed the service.

I was admitted to the hospital for the third and final time. I didn't want to go back, but my condition had been going on for a long time, and it was only getting worse. I felt tired and frustrated; this was the first time I gave in to the condition of this extreme. I felt hopeless, accepting, and believing that things wouldn't change. Everyone had their lives to live; my siblings had to go to school or work, and my parents had to work. I couldn't manage to stay by myself anymore, and I saw myself as a burden to everyone. I told my mom just to let them admit me into the hospital. She saw the situation but didn't know I had given up. So, she brought me to the clinic and asked them to admit me, and they did.

Stigma Attached to Mental Illness

It was difficult to live a normal life, especially with the stigma attached to mental illness. Society often stigmatizes persons who suffers from mental illnesses because they believe they will cause trouble. Historically, they used to lock them away in mental institutions because they couldn't do anything else to protect people with mental health conditions from harming themselves or others. Despite my condition, I only wanted to return to school, achieve something, and be a normal part of society. I craved a sense of normalcy. I tried going back to various schools to complete a course in early childhood education, but due to my illness, they told me not to return to the institutions. Not because I was harming anyone but because of the panic attacks. I was viewed as a liability. Imagine people without social support; then, society closes the doors in their faces. This leaves one feeling like they don't belong, allowing the voice "You don't belong; you are a burden to others; you're not wanted; just end it all" to consume them. This kind of alienation greatly affects the soul.

> **"** *Despite my condition, I only wanted to return to school, achieve something, and be a normal part of society. I craved a sense of normalcy.*
> *Let's say, for instance, that I was mentally ill and was on medications and behaving "normal." Shouldn't that be enough for me to be accepted? Or was society trying to say I was still an outcast when my behavior was stable?*

In January 2021, the final school I attended was the National College of Professional Studies to complete a course in practical nursing. While attending the course and matters were moving smoothly, I heard my classmates who lived within my community and knew of my past went ahead and told the principal, my teacher, and other students what to expect from me and what I've been through. When I went on work experience, my supervisor knew me before I even got there. Society fought against me, expecting the worst, and tried to fail me before giving me a fair chance to excel. Let's say, for instance, that I was mentally ill and was on medications and behaving "normal." Shouldn't that be enough for me to be accepted? Or, was society trying to say I was still an outcast when my behavior was stable? Society seems to see the worst in people, even when the best is on display. They tried to make me feel like I wasn't good enough to be a part of society like I would never achieve anything. It seems that when a person has encountered a battle with the mind, your life ends there, and there is no way of returning. If I had waited for society to validate me, I would be locked in my room for years, looking through the window and wondering when they would have given me a chance.

> *Society fought against me, expecting the worst, and tried to fail me before giving me a fair chance to excel.*
> *Society seems to see the worst in people, even when the best is on display.*
> *If I had waited for society to validate me, I would be locked in my room for years, looking through the window and wondering when they would have given me a chance.*

Suicide is a common problem in society at large. According to recorded data by the Jamaica Constabulary Force (JCF), suicidal statistics reveal that men have committed suicide more than women since the year 2000. Between the years 2000 and 2019, 1,008 cases of suicide have been reported, with men accounting for 84 percent of that figure. This translates to 844 men whose deaths have been by suicide, senior communications strategist for the JCF, Dennis Brooks, told the Jamaica Observer, in contrast to 164 women" (Francis, 2021). According to Gleaner (2023), "the latest Jamaican figures were published in the Economic and Social Survey of Jamaica, which the Planning Institute of Jamaica recently released. According to the report, 64 suicides were recorded in 2022, moving up from 51 in 2021. Males accounted for 90.6 percent of victims." The Minister of Health & Wellness, Dr. The Hon. Christopher Tufton (2020), said, "While Jamaica's suicide rate has remained low when compared to many other countries, we cannot become complacent. We are aware that health systems and society present risk factors for suicide. They include barriers to accessing health care, inappropriate media reporting on cases of suicide, access to means of committing suicide, and stigma associated with help-seeking behavior."

The World Health Organization (WHO) has reported that more than 700,000 people die by suicide each year, which is one person every 40 seconds. WHO further reported that suicide is a global phenomenon and occurs throughout the lifespan. There are indications, WHO said, which show that for each adult who died by suicide, there may have been more than 20 others attempting suicide (Francis, 2021). Dr Donovan Thomas, a local suicidologist, mentioned in a few articles published by the Jamaica Gleaner that one person around the world commits suicide every 40 seconds (Murphy, 2020). Pan American Health Organization United Nations Development Programme (2019) statistics show around 3% of Jamaicans have a depressive disorder and 4.1% have an anxiety disorder. Women are at a disproportionate risk for both disorders, as 3.7% have depression and 4.3% have anxiety, compared to just 2.3% of men for each disorder. These statistical numbers tell us that we have work to do as a society to support those facing mental health challenges.

There are so many persons struggling with feelings of depression or hopelessness, which has called attention to mental health and suicide prevention. Persons need to know it is okay to have a bad day or a few bad days. It is okay to feel down; it is natural for human beings. It is also okay to express how you feel to someone. Do not allow depression to consume you. We should be able to identify when a situation is beyond normal and when we need help to manage it. A mental crisis or breakdown of your mental health is a situation where you experience intense physical and emotional distress and find it difficult to cope and function effectively. The support from family members, friends, community, co-workers, classmates, and everyone in general is important. People struggling with mental health need listening ears. Society needs to normalize people expressing emotions about bad days, negative thoughts, and daily challenges. We need compassion, empathy, uplifting, positive words, and encouragement to face challenges and empowerment to overcome them. More importantly, we need a solid relationship with God so that the Holy Spirit can empower us to navigate life's challenges.

> Persons need to know it is okay to have a bad day or a few bad days. It is okay to feel down; it is natural for human beings. It is also okay to express how you feel to someone.
> We should be able to identify when a situation is beyond normal and when we need help to manage it.
> People struggling with mental health need listening ears. Society needs to normalize people expressing emotions about bad days, negative thoughts, and daily challenges.

Some persons might say, "I would never commit suicide; I could never be so depressed to be admitted into a hospital." However, as Paul writes in 1 Corinthians 10:12, the reality is, "Therefore let him who thinks he stands take heed lest he fall." As such, let us be empathetic and compassionate to those who experience mental health issues. My family pastor, Rev. Windel Daley, visited me when I was admitted to the hospital and a few times at my home. He told my mom and I that I didn't have a mental illness, but he didn't want to tell me directly to stop taking medications. The side effects of the medications caused me to gain approximately sixty-five pounds within a year. I recall persons I knew from past schools asking me if I was pregnant when they saw me. As I walked in Mandeville or other parishes, taxi men would call out to me, "Baby mother! You ready!" Recently, a psychiatric nurse aide that stayed with us during my admission saw my mother in Mandeville and stopped her. While inquiring on my well-being, she asked my mother how my baby was doing. My mother had to inform her that I was not pregnant. I gained weight mostly in my stomach area, so I appeared as if I was pregnant. The side effects of the medication also caused me to experience poor memory, poor vision, and temporarily produce milk from my breast. The psychiatrist kept on increasing my medications to the highest dosage because she didn't understand why I kept on experiencing severe panic attacks, anxiety, depression and hallucination, that resulted in frequent hospital admissions.

The increased medications made me feel sleepy, lethargic, and moved extremely slowly. The visitation from my pastor restored my hope for recovery and a breakthrough. Sometimes, we encounter situations that our loved ones and friends witness, but unfortunately, they cannot remedy the condition. Not even finances can correct the situation. Just like the woman with the issue of blood for twelve years in Luke 8:43-48, no physicians nor money could have remedied the situation. All it took was for her to extend her faith in Jesus and reached out to Him for restoration and healing. I followed her footsteps and reached out to Jesus for my deliverance, healing, and restoration.

Hospital Visitation

> " The visitation from my pastor restored my hope for recovery and a breakthrough.
> Just like the woman with the issue of blood for twelve years in Luke 8:43-48, no physicians nor money could have remedied the situation. All it took was for her to extend her faith in Jesus and reached out to Him for restoration and healing. I followed her footsteps and reached out to Jesus for my deliverance, healing, and restoration.

A Sound Mind

Photo taken by sister, Shanniel Richards on April 3, 2019 at the mental health clinic at the Mandeville Comprehensive Clinic, accompanied by nephew, Christiano Richards.

Hospital Visitation

Shannese after coming from church in 2020, approximately 1 year after being on psychotropic medications.

"The optimist sees the glass as half full, the pessimist as half empty. What I see is water that can save someone's life."

— ABHIJIT NASKAR

Chapter 5

Power of the Mind

The mind is one of the most powerful human faculties. The mind plays a critical role in the biblical framework. It plays a major role in governing our lives and directing our decisions. As Christians, our goal is to have the mind of Jesus Christ. Paul exhorts us in Philippians 2:5 to let the mind of Christ be in us. According to gotquestions.org, "having the mind of Christ means sharing the plan, purpose, and perspective of Christ, and is something that all believers possess." Having the mind of Christ means thinking like Jesus did, as revealed in the synoptic gospels, so we can act like He did. It is imperative for us to study the teachings of Jesus to learn about His thinking, plan, purpose, and perspective. When we think like Jesus, we identify with His mission to glorify God and to bring souls into His kingdom.

Power of the Mind

> *Having the mind of Christ means thinking like Jesus did, as revealed in the synoptic gospels, so we can act like He did. When we think like Jesus, we identify with His mission to glorify God and to bring souls into His kingdom.*

Gotquestion.org points out some very important truths concerning the mind of Christ in 1 Corinthians 2. First, the mind of Christ contradicts man's wisdom (verses 5-6). Divine operations often diametrically oppose human operations. God's ways and thoughts are not like human ways and thoughts—they are higher and in alignment with God's sovereign plan for humanity. The eagle-eye prophet Isaiah writes, "For My thoughts are not your thoughts, nor are your ways My ways," says the Lord. As the heavens are higher than the earth, so are My ways higher than your ways, and My thoughts than your thoughts" (Isaiah 55:8-9). God chose a shepherd boy, David, to be the next king of Israel and not Jesse's other sons, who appeared militant, physically capable, and qualified to lead a nation in warfare. God looks at the heart and not outward appearance like we tend to do (see 1 Samuel 16:7). God sees and hears on a level that we don't. God chose preaching as the instrument to win souls into His kingdom. God allowed Joseph to be sold into slavery by his brothers to eventually be promoted to prime minister of Egypt after several unfortunate turn of events to save Joseph's family and the preservation of Israel. God chose faith in Christ as the means of salvation, not our own works or merits. What God deems as wise is foolishness to the natural mind. What we deem as wise is foolishness to God.

> *Divine operations often diametrically oppose human operations.*
> *God's ways and thoughts are not like human ways and thoughts—they are higher and in alignment with God's sovereign plan for humanity.*
> *What God deems as wise is foolishness to the natural mind. What we deem as wise is foolishness to God.*

Second, the mind of Christ involves wisdom from God, which was once hidden but now revealed (verse 7). We see God's wisdom in Christ's life and His victory over His enemies despite His sufferings. Third, the mind of Christ is given to believers through the spirit of God (verses 10-12). The manner of impartation of spiritual knowledge is through revelation by the Holy Spirit. God is in the business of revealing things that can only be unveiled through His Spirit. We need to recognize the leading of the Holy Spirit in our lives to tap into divine revelations. Fourth, those without the Spirit of God cannot understand the mind of Christ. Paul writes in 1 Corinthians 2:14, "But the natural man does not receive the things of the Spirit of God, for they are foolishness to him; nor can he know them, because they are spiritually discerned." Spiritual things are spiritually discerned. As such, a natural-minded person cannot understand spiritual things. Only regenerated persons can understand the things of God. Lastly, the mind of Christ gives believers discernment in spiritual matters (verse 15). Believers in Christ can test the spirits—distinguishing between what is of God, what is of humans, and what is of Satan and demons. We get the mind of Christ by placing our faith in Jesus and His finished work on Calvary, which gives the Holy Spirit latitude to indwell, lead, and direct our lives, thus enlightening us with divine wisdom.

> We see God's wisdom in Christ's life and His victory over His enemies despite His sufferings.
> We need to recognize the leading of the Holy Spirit in our lives to tap into divine revelations.

Three Types of People

From a biblical perspective, there are three types of people—natural-minded, spiritually-minded, and carnal-minded. Mills (2011) pointed out the difference between these three types of people. First, he stated, "a natural-minded person is governed by their sensory mechanisms. Such a person operates in this world based on what they can perceive. A natural-minded person does not understand the ways of God." Natural-minded people do not have the mind of Christ or the Holy Spirit dwelling inside them. The natural mind relies on intellect, human knowledge, and human wisdom rather than spiritual insights.

In contrast, Mills stated about the carnal-minded person:

> "The flesh governs a carnal-minded person. Such a person may believe there is a God but refuse to allow the Holy Spirit to govern their life. Such a person puts the object of their faith in their own ability, strength, education, religious effort, etc., to receive victory from God. Such a person gravitates toward the oldness of the letter (law) rather than the newness of the spirit (the Holy Spirit). The end result is defeat."

Romans 8:6-7 states, "To be carnally minded is death, but to be spiritually minded is life and peace. Because the carnal mind is enmity against God; for it is not subject to the law of God, nor indeed can be." This passage emphasizes that a carnal mind is enmity—deep-seated mutual hatred—towards God. Henceforth, at no point in life can a carnal mind please God. The carnal mind is indicative of the flesh. As Christians, we were not called to walk by feelings or our senses but solely by faith. Hebrews 11:6 says, "But without faith, it is impossible to please Him..." The New International Version puts it this way,

"The mind governed by the flesh is hostile to God; it does not submit to God's law, nor can it do so. Those in the realm of the flesh cannot please God." To this end, Diaz (2022) points out, "The scripture clearly states that a carnal mind is dominated by selfishness. It's the mind that is self-willed, self-focused, and self-seeking. The carnal mind is devoid of the ability to surrender wholeheartedly to God." Mitchel (2022) echoes the same sentiments: "To change from a carnal mind to a spiritual mind, we need to follow God's plan of salvation, including being baptized for the remission of our sins and to read and study the Bible daily. This will give us a new mindset, renewing our minds from worldly to spiritual ones."

Lastly, Mills pointed out the difference with the spiritually minded person:

> "The spiritually minded person puts the object of his faith exclusively in the cross of Christ. This gives the Holy Spirit latitude to work in their life. Sin no longer has dominion over them. Such a person knows their position in Christ and walks by faith, not sight. Such a person's spiritual transmission is always tuned to Heaven's frequency—God's instructions and divine interventions. Such a person is not governed by his sensory mechanisms; instead, he is governed by the Holy Spirit. The end result is perpetual victory."

Being spiritually minded means allowing Christ's teachings to direct, dominate, and guide our thoughts, govern our emotions, and control our spoken words and actions. To be spiritually minded, we must stay focused on God to overcome adverse circumstances or situations. The Bible comforts us in 1 Peter 5:7 by instructing us, "casting all your care upon Him [Jesus], for He cares for you." God is full of compassion towards us. In casting our worries or concerns upon Him, He releases our anxiety and fears. God requires constant, daily communication with Him to condition our minds to conform to His sovereign will. Although He sees what we are going through, He wants us to build a relationship with Him by telling Him what we are going through.

> *Although He sees what we are going through, He wants us to build a relationship with Him by telling Him what we are going through.*

After the fall of Adam and Eve in Genesis 3:9-12, God showed up. He called Adam and asked, "Where are you?" God is omniscient; He knew where Adam was. However, He wanted to have a relationship with Adam and Eve despite their fall. We can rest assured that God also wants to establish and maintain a relationship with us. Trust is an integral part of this relationship. We are exhorted in Proverbs 3:5-6 to "Trust in the Lord with all your heart and lean not on your own understanding; In all your ways acknowledge Him, and He shall direct your paths." God is often depicted as a counselor (Psalm 16:7; 32:8; 33:11; 73:24) who encourages and strengthens us along life's journey. Through constant communication with Him, He will help us to overcome depression, anxiety, stress, loss, and relationship difficulties that affect our lives.

The Bible encourages us to redirect our minds from worldly things and to renew our minds towards godly things. Paul writes in Romans 12:2, "do not be conformed to this world, but be transformed by the renewing of your mind, that you may prove what is that good and acceptable and perfect will of God." To protect our renewed minds, the Bible reminds us to put on the full armor of God, including the helmet of salvation, which assures us of eternal life and guards us against spiritual assaults. Biblical meditation helps us to direct our thoughts on the things of God. Paul suggests things we ought to meditate on in Philippians 4:8: "Finally, brethren, whatever things are true, whatever things are noble, whatever things are just, whatever things are pure, whatever things are lovely, whatever things are of good report, if there is any virtue and if there is anything praiseworthy—meditate on these things." According to Mills (2008), "biblical meditation is an attempt to empty our minds of wrong thinking in order to fill our minds with rightful thinking according to God's Word. It involves reflective thinking on biblical truths so that God can speak to us through His Word and the thoughts that come to our minds. Christian meditation aims to internalize and personalize the scripture so that its truth can affect our attitudes and actions and how we think and live." This type of meditation is chewing on God's Words so that we may bear godly fruits in our lives.

Scientific Perspective of the Mind

There is a distinction between the brain, a human organism, and the mind. According to the Johns Hopkins School of Medicine, "the brain is a complex organ that controls thought, memory, emotion, touch, motor skills, vision, breathing, temperature, hunger, and every process that regulates our body. The brain and spinal cord that extends from it comprise the central nervous system." Much of our physical existence is directed from the brain. Interestingly, the brain is a small organ weighing only about three pounds in the average adult. It is about 60% fat; the remaining 40% combines water, protein, carbohydrates, and salts (John Hopkins School of Medicine).

On the other hand, the mind is a spiritual aspect of the physical brain. Gifford (2022) elaborates,

> "The mind, described in Romans 12:2, goes beyond mere thoughts. It encompasses our way of thinking, attitude, and the sum total of our mental and moral state of being. The brain, on the other hand, is a tangible, organic organ within the human anatomy. It is observable and physical. When the Bible mentions the brain, it refers to our outer person or body. This distinction is evident from passages throughout Scripture, from the account of creation (Genesis 2:7) to discussions about life and death (2 Corinthians 5:8-9). Our outer person (including the brain) experiences physical decay, while our inner person (mind) should be continually renewed (2 Corinthians 4:16-18)."

Sigmund Freud is known by many in the scientific community as the father of psychoanalysis primarily because of his psychoanalytical theory. He was the first person to develop a model of the mind. Freud's theory of the mind shaped how psychologists, psychiatrists, and psychoanalysts viewed the human mind and personality. In 1923, Freud created the model of the mind that is presently utilized: the unconscious, preconscious or subconscious, and conscious minds. He also developed a theory of personality involving the Id, ego, and superego. These three elements work together to create complex human behaviors. The Id operates on an unconscious level and focuses solely on instinctual desires like survival. The ego's function is to keep the Id in check to ensure it adapts to acceptable social norms and conditions. It operates on a conscious level. The superego focuses on morality and higher principles. It operates on the unconscious and preconscious levels (Byers, 2022).

According to Freud, the unconscious mind holds thoughts and feelings that cannot be easily accessed. This implies that unconscious thoughts and desires drive our behaviors. This part of the mind also holds repressed and suppressed traumas and painful emotions. It is also viewed as a storage for thoughts, memories, and knowledge that are no longer useful. Our long-term memories are stored in the preconscious or subconscious mind, holding all the mental processes we are unaware of. The conscious mind is where our current thoughts and feelings reside. This includes everything we are aware of and relates to short-term memory. This part of the mind also controls logical and critical thinking (Byers, 2022).

The Spiritual Mind

In Philippians 4:6-7, Paul writes, "Be anxious for nothing, but in everything by prayer and supplication, with thanksgiving, let your requests be made known to God; and the peace of God, which surpasses all understanding, will guard your hearts and minds through Christ Jesus." Anxious thoughts and feelings are not God's will for our lives. They reflect a lack of faith and trust in God. Whenever we think or feel anxious, we should seek God in prayer. We should view them as indicators that we need to pray. This can be a simple prayer like, "I bring these anxious thoughts under subjection to the power of the Holy Spirit in Jesus' name. Let God's will be done for my life. I trust God."

> " Whenever we think or feel anxious, we should seek God in prayer. We should view them as indicators that we need to pray.

We are seeking to redirect our thoughts and feelings to the knowledge and power of God working in and through us by the power of the Holy Spirit. Doing so means God is more powerful and significant than anxious thoughts and feelings. God promises to give us peace and direction in all situations or circumstances that may be overwhelming or out of our control. After all, we believe in God's sovereignty that He will overrule or override all matters to align with the counsel of His will. No situation or circumstance is out of the purview of an all-seeing and all-knowing God. This supernatural peace from Christ surpasses the understanding of the carnal or natural mind, for it is spiritually minded.

> We are seeking to redirect our thoughts and feelings to the knowledge and power of God working in and through us by the power of the Holy Spirit. Doing so means God is more powerful and significant than anxious thoughts and feelings.
> No situation or circumstance is out of the purview of an all-seeing and all-knowing God.

God reassures us in John 14:27, "Peace I leave with you, my peace I give to you; not as the world gives do I give to you. Let not your heart be troubled, neither let it be afraid." As born-again children of the Most High God, we receive supernatural peace, but we need to walk in this peace by abiding in Christ and His Word. This is an unexplainable peace—a calmness from the assurance that God oversees all matters—deriving from the in-dwelling Holy Spirit. We are required to be spiritually minded by fixing our focused-on God and not on ourselves, on other people, or on our circumstances and situations. The Holy Spirit will remove doubts and worries. He will deliver us from fears that prompt panic attacks and anxiety.

1 John 4:18 tells us, "There is no fear in love, but perfect love casts out fear because fear involves torment. But he who fears has not been made perfect in love. We love Him because He first loved us." As believers, we believe that God loves us. He has chosen us to play a role in His divine plan for humanity. We can rest in this love even during our darkest days, knowing all is well with our souls. All that is in the world that we seek peace and comfort in, whether drugs, alcohol, or sex, cannot be compared to the peace that Jesus gives. The world produces deceptive and temporary peace, but after worldly peace wears off, we experience torment. God's love overpowers fear when we experience His perfect love. It leaves no place for fear in our minds, hearts, and lives. The assurance of God's love enables us to face life's challenges. Whenever I was disturbed by negative thoughts, I read God's Word, which eventually brought peace and comfort to my mind.

We must depend on the Holy Spirit to guide us in prayer as He searches our hearts and intercedes on our behalf. "Likewise, the Spirit also helps in our weaknesses. For we do not know what we should pray for as we ought, but the Spirit Himself makes intercession for us with groanings which cannot be uttered" (Romans 8:26). So, even when situations and circumstances consume us. We don't know how to pray; the Holy Spirit intercedes on our behalf with deep expressions beyond words.

Also, we can conquer depression by abiding in the presence of the Holy Spirit. In God's presence, there is fullness of joy (Psalm 16:11). Depression cannot remain when we tap into the joy of our Lord. The joy of the Lord is our strength (see Nehemiah 8:10).

A strong mind empowered by the Holy Spirit can help us navigate the vicissitudes of life. It can help us overcome obstacles and challenges that could otherwise destroy us. This is one reason the enemy often targets our minds. The enemy is quite aware that he can obstruct the path God has for us if he can disturb our minds. Gotquestions.org defines the mind from a biblical perspective as, 'the 'inner being' or the sum total of all our mental, emotional, and spiritual faculties, without drawing fine distinctions between them." The concept of "inner being" as a definition of the mind is interesting because it taps into the core of who we are. This part of us defines and shapes our character and chart the course of our lives. There is a significant correlation between what happens in our inner beings and accomplishing our God-given destinies in this life. The enemy seems to create turmoil in our inner being to derail our lives from God's path.

Speak Words of Life

Proverbs 16:32 states, "He who is slow to anger is better than the mighty, and he who rules his spirit than he who takes a city." The Bible emphasizes that the power to control the mind is better than a powerful warrior who rules a city. Many mighty men can fight wars, but the war we fight in our minds is often one we fight alone. Many people are silently struggling with mental health issues. They often feel isolated because of the stigma attached to mental illness. Consequently, they bottle-up or suppress negative emotions and thoughts that can later become disastrous. The enemy tends to plant negative thoughts in our minds, especially when we are alone. The more we listen to negative thoughts, the louder the voices become. Negative thoughts may swirl around in our heads such as "you're a mistake; you aren't enough; you're a failure; you're a burden to others; you should just kill yourself." Those thoughts are all lies from the enemy to derail or destroy our lives. Everyone encounters negative thoughts, especially when alone, but those suffering from mental illnesses face more challenges and setbacks in life. We should make it a habit to speak positive thoughts over our lives—words of life. Words of affirmation will encourage us to continue the good fight of faith and see the glass half full rather than half empty. Some of these positive thoughts are, "I can do all things through Christ who strengthens me; I am more than a conqueror through Christ Jesus; I am intelligent; I will accomplish my God-given destiny by God's grace."

> Many mighty men can fight wars, but the war we fight in our minds is often one we fight alone.
> We should make it a habit to speak positive thoughts over our lives—words of life. Words of affirmation will encourage us to continue the good fight of faith and see the glass half full rather than half empty.

Over time, we become the product of our innermost thoughts, which ultimately define us in some way, shape, or form. Proverbs 23:7 states, "For as he thinks in his heart, so is he." How can we think in our hearts? There is a mind-heart connection where thoughts originate and flow from our hearts. This is why it is important to guard the gates of our hearts, for out of them flow the issues of life (Proverbs 4:23). Our heart gates are our eyes and ears. We must be careful what our eyes and ears are fixed on because they will influence our thoughts. Our thoughts and beliefs produce our actions, which eventually shape our character.

> We must be careful what our eyes and ears are fixed on because they will influence our thoughts.

After entertaining negative thoughts and starting to believe them, they began to control the narrative of my life. When my mind realized that those negative thoughts were overtaking my mental space, those thoughts became demanding, forcefully telling me what to do. Some of the things I was told to do were to isolate myself and watch depressing videos, listen to depressing songs, and read sad quotes. I then began to act upon the things I fed my mind, so I became depressed and consumed with sadness. My thoughts, words, actions, and desires were depressing. It felt like being underwater, drowning in depression, but my soul was crying out for rescue. Most individuals focused on only the outward display of my mental challenges but did not consider that I needed genuine help and support. It appeared that they didn't consider that I was also a human being with a dying soul and needed someone to hear the cry of my soul and know I was still alive inside.

> *Most individuals focused on only the outward display of my mental challenges but did not consider that I needed genuine help and support. It appeared that they didn't consider that I was also a human being with a dying soul and needed someone to hear the cry of my soul and know I was still alive inside.*

Individuals witnessed that I was losing control of my mind and being manipulated by the enemy; they saw a warfare they could not handle. They recognized I was losing the war over my mind, and some thought I had already completely lost it. Instead of helping me from the outside by tapping into the spiritual realm and speaking words of breakthrough, they ignorantly joined forces with the enemy by slandering my name, attaching "mad" or "mentally ill" to it. The negative words from both within my mind and people were destroying me. Sometimes, we tend to forget how powerful words are. God reminded us in Isaiah 55:11 of the power and effectiveness of words. He mentioned, "So shall My word be that goes forth from My mouth; It shall not return to Me void, but it shall accomplish what I please, and it shall prosper in the thing for which I sent it." Proverbs 18:21 also reminds us about the power of words: "Death and life are in the power of the tongue, and those who love it will eat its fruit." Instead of saying the mentally ill girl, people could have cried out, "Have mercy, Lord," or "give her more grace" or "the blood of Jesus," or just called on the name of Jesus every time they remembered me. They would have spoken words of deliverance into the atmosphere. Isaiah 59:1 declares, "The Lord's hand is not shortened, that it cannot save; nor His ear heavy, that it cannot hear." God wanted to deliver me, but the forces against me were multiplying and gaining traction in the spirit realm. Ultimately, we will see that God won but wanted His people in the spirit of community to learn to unite around a cause—delivering one of His children. People handed me over to mental illness, but God said I permitted it so that the power of the Holy Spirit might be displayed through me.

> " *God wanted to deliver me, but the forces against me were multiplying and gaining traction in the spirit realm. Ultimately, we will see that God won but wanted His people in the spirit of community to learn to unite around a cause—delivering one of His children.*
> *People handed me over to mental illness, but God said I permitted it so that the power of the Holy Spirit might be displayed through me.*

Demonic oppression and possession are serious matters recorded in the Bible. While Christians can be oppressed or influenced by demonic spirits, they cannot be possessed by them because of the indwelling Holy Spirit. Luke 8:26-36 records an account of Jesus encountering and casting out demons from a man and healing his soul in the country of the Gadarenes. This man was possessed for a long time, wore no clothes, was tormented, exhibited self-destructive behaviors, and lived in the tombs. However, when this man saw Jesus, he cried out, fell down before Him, and with a loud voice said, "What have I to do with You, Jesus, Son of the Most High God? I beg You, do not torment me!" (verse 28). The demons were speaking through this man. Note carefully that the demons knew who Jesus was and feared Him. When Jesus commanded the demons to leave the man, they begged Him that He would not cast them into the abyss (verse 31). Jesus then permitted the demons to enter a herd of swine, who then ran violently into a lake and drowned. Jesus demonstrated that He had power over demonic spirits, so we can rest assured that we can experience deliverance and healing from demonic oppression or possession.

> " While Christians can be oppressed or influenced by demonic spirits, they cannot be possessed by them because of the indwelling Holy Spirit.
> Jesus demonstrated that He had power over demonic spirits, so we can rest assured that we can experience deliverance and healing from demonic oppression or possession.

The devil's voice is loud, forceful, and pushy. On the contrary, the voice of God is a still, small voice leading us to green pastures. Matthew 4:1 explains the operation of the Holy Spirit, where the Spirit led Jesus into the wilderness. Even when God speaks to us to do something for our good, He speaks in a way that doesn't interfere with our willpower, allowing us to make decisions independently. On the contrary, the devil is ready to condemn us, speaking in a manner to overpower our will, thereby gaining control over our choices. We need to distinguish the voice of God from the enemies' voice so we can ignore the enemy's voice or counteract it with the Word of God. When we ignore the enemy's voice, the volume will turn down until it eventually fades away. James 4:7 assures us, "Submit to God. Resist the devil, and he will flee from you."

> Even when God speaks to us to do something for our good, He speaks in a way that doesn't interfere with our willpower, allowing us to make decisions independently. On the contrary, the devil is ready to condemn us, speaking in a manner to overpower our will, thereby gaining control over our choices.
> We need to distinguish the voice of God from the enemies' voice so we can ignore the enemy's voice or counteract it with the Word of God. When we ignore the enemy's voice, the volume will turn down until it eventually fades away.

The Word of God teaches us to be aware that there is spiritual warfare where we wrestle against principalities, powers, rulers of the darkness of this age, and spiritual hosts of wickedness in heavenly places (Ephesians 6:12). 2 Corinthians 10:5 (KJV) further tells us that there is a warfare that takes place within the mind: "Casting down imaginations, and every high thing that exalts itself against the knowledge of God and bringing into captivity every thought to the obedience of Christ." This verse teaches us the importance of recognizing and immediately pulling down negative thoughts or imaginations before they form as strongholds, renouncing and denouncing negative thoughts within our minds, and aligning our thoughts and actions with the Word of God.

As Christians, we are strengthened when we spend quality time nurturing the mind of Christ in us. This kind of mindset helps us to support each other with life's myriad challenges. 2 Philippians 2:5 tells us, "Let this mind be in you which was also in Christ Jesus." The idea is to have the same mindset that Christ had. Christ was willing to humble Himself and give up His glory by becoming a man and dying on the cross for sinful humans, though He was sinless (see Philippians 2:7-8). Jesus is the supreme example of love and humility because He gave Himself up as an expression of love and was willing to lower Himself to express that love. Paul challenges us to think like Jesus by lowering ourselves for the benefit of others. We can only agree with Christ by maintaining the same love, expressing His purposes, and having a bold willingness to make our own interests and purposes subservient to the greater good of others. Let us, therefore, lower ourselves and help each other in the fight against mental illness.

> *Jesus is the supreme example of love and humility because He gave Himself up as an expression of love and was willing to lower Himself to express that love.*
> *We can only agree with Christ by maintaining the same love, expressing His purposes, and having a bold willingness to make our own interests and purposes subservient to the greater good of others. Let us, therefore, lower ourselves and help each other in the fight against mental illness.*
> *Paul challenges us to think like Jesus by lowering ourselves for the benefit of others.*

"Faith does not mean trusting God to stop the storm but trusting Him to strengthen us as we walk through the storm."

- Anonymous

Chapter 6

Spiritual Warfare – Efforts To Destroy Our "Stars"

The Purpose of Altars

Altars are very significant in spiritual warfare. They serve as points of contact where human beings connect with divinity or evil entities in the spirit realm. They activate power in the spirit realm and can be used for benevolent and malevolent reasons. Baker's Evangelical Dictionary of Biblical Theology defines an altar as "a structure on which offerings are made to a deity." The Hebrew word for altar is "mizbeah," from a verbal root meaning "to slaughter." The Greek word for altar is "thusiasterion," meaning "a place of sacrifice." In Old Testament theology, an altar is a place where sacrifices were offered to God. God requested His people to sacrifice unto Him to cover their sins. Sacrifices in the Old Testament foreshadow the perfect sacrifice of the Lamb of God, Jesus Christ. Without the shedding of blood, there is no remission of sins (see Hebrews

9:22). This was God's system of dealing with humanity's sin problem. Other sacrifices, such as grain, fruit, wine, and incense were also used. God smelled the aroma from the burnt sacrifices and granted the request of those who built altars if He was pleased. The idea of an altar was introduced in Genesis 4:1-5 where Cain and Abel brought their sacrifices unto God. Abel brought an offering—fat portions from some of the firstborn of his flock—and God accepted his offering. Cain brought some of the fruits of the soil as an offering. God rejected his offering. It is important to note that Abel's sacrifice was a type and foreshadowing of the sacrifice of Jesus Christ.

> Altars serve as points of contact where human beings connect with divinity or evil entities in the spirit realm. They activate power in the spirit realm and can be used for benevolent and malevolent reasons.

In Christianity, an altar is a sacred place within an edifice or temple where believers connect with God. This is a physical structure or consecrated place where believers meet with God to offer thanksgiving, sacrifice, worship, prayer, and to cry out in vulnerability. Under the new covenant, our bodies and hearts are sacrificed to God. Paul writes in Romans 1:12 to "offer our bodies as a living sacrifice, holy and pleasing to God. This is our true and proper worship." Sacrifice is defined as anything consecrated and offered to God. God doesn't expect us to sacrifice our physical bodies by cutting ourselves on church altars, or to sacrifice animals as the Mosaic Law required, but to offer ourselves as a living sacrifice. We ought to cleanse ourselves through constant confession and repentance and surrender ourselves completely and wholeheartedly to God, allowing Him to use us as a vessel to do His will. An altar is also a place where a covenant is made. After a pastor finish preaching a sermon and makes "an altar call," he extends an invitation to the congregation to come to the altar if they accept Jesus Christ as their personal Lord and Savior, trusting in His death as the final payment for their sins and His resurrection as their guarantee of eternal life. When people respond by saying "yes," they immediately make a covenant by faith—an agreement with God—where the Holy Spirit resides in their spirits, leading them into all truth.

Under the new covenant, we no longer depend on a high priest to annually offer animals as offerings for our sins. Jesus is our Great High Priest who paid the sin debt in full for those who believe and trust in Him as Lord and Savior. We can confidently approach God's throne of grace to receive mercy and find grace in our time of need (Hebrews 4:14-16, NIV). Jesus' shed blood on Calvary's Cross puts us in right standing with God, the Father. He also makes intercession on our behalf. This biblical doctrine is referred to as justification by faith in Christ alone. Hebrews 9:12-13 states, "Not with the blood of goats and calves, but with His [Jesus'] own blood He entered the Most Holy Place once for all, having obtained eternal redemption."

> " Jesus is our Great High Priest who paid the sin debt in full for those who believe and trust in Him as Lord and Savior. Jesus' shed blood on Calvary's Cross puts us in right standing with God, the Father. He also makes intercession on our behalf.

Altars open spiritual portals. The Oxford Dictionary defines a portal as "a doorway, gate, or other entrance." Genesis 28:11-19 clearly shows that an altar opens spiritual portals. As Jacob travelled from Beersheba and went toward Haran, he tarried at a certain place all night. He took a stone from that place, put them on his pillows, laid down, and slept. As he slept, he dreamt that he saw a ladder set up on the earth, and the top of it reached heaven, where he saw the angels of God ascending and descending on it. The Lord stood above it and introduced Himself as the Lord God of Abraham and Isaac, thus reaffirming the covenant made with his forefathers. The land where Jacob laid would be given to him and his descendants, and through them, all families on earth would be blessed. When Jacob awoke, he recognized that the place where he sleeps is sacred and declared in verse 17 that he is in the house of God. In gratitude and reverence, Jacob took the stone he had used as a pillow and set it up as a pillar or altar. He anointed it by pouring oil on the top of it. The stone represented an altar, a place of worship and connection with God.

Scripture makes it clear that God was the one who initiated the idea of an altar. This was God's way of bridging the divide between Himself and humanity resulting from the fall. In contrast to divine or godly altars, there are evil or diabolic altars. Godly altars are meant for us to reconcile with God and bless His people, while evil altars are meant to curse, afflict, and destroy persons, thus hindering them from fulfilling their divine purposes and destinies. In other words, evil altars are "destiny alters"—they are meant to change the course of one's destiny. According to The King's Parish, "a diabolic altar is a high place, shrine, occultic center, a place of meeting between men and spirits – a place of contact with the spirit world, a place of sacrifice and invocation of evil spirits. It's a place to monitor people's progress and to control people. Manifestations of satanic altars include delayed blessings, periodic sicknesses, irritational behavior, suicidal tendencies, abnormal losses, inexplicable discouragements, mysterious body marks, terrible nightmares, suspicion." (The Kings Parish, 2021).

Spiritual Warfare – Efforts To Destroy Our "Stars"

> " Godly altars are meant for us to reconcile with God and bless His people, while evil altars are meant to curse, afflict, and destroy persons, thus hindering them from fulfilling their divine purposes and destinies.
> Evil altars are "destiny alters"—they are meant to change the course of one's destiny.

We were all born with a "star" representing our God-given destiny in this lifetime. We are meant to travel a certain trajectory throughout our earthly lives. Evil altars locate that "star" in the spirit realm and seek to alter or destroy it before it can manifest. This is important to Satan because he knows if we accomplish our God-given destinies, his kingdom will be threatened, and his evil plans will be dismantled. This creates much tension in our lives, both spiritually and naturally, as Satan works nonstop with his demonic kingdom to destroy God's purposes. Matthew 11:12 tells us, "And from the time of John the Baptist began preaching until now, the Kingdom of Heaven has been forcefully advancing, and violent people are attacking it." A main characteristic of Satan and his demons is violent attacks. They attack God's people and purposes through forces of darkness, such as various forms of witchcraft and black magic. Their goal is to stop the kingdom of God from advancing so that the kingdom of darkness can prevail.

A Sound Mind

> " We were all born with a "star" representing our God-given destiny in this lifetime. Evil altars locate that "star" in the spirit realm and seek to alter or destroy it before it can manifest. This is important to Satan because he knows if we accomplish our God-given destinies, his kingdom will be threatened, and his evil plans will be dismantled.
>
> A main characteristic of Satan and his demons is violent attacks. They attack God's people and purposes through forces of darkness, such as various forms of witchcraft and black magic. Their goal is to stop the kingdom of God from advancing so that the kingdom of darkness can prevail.

Satan sought to destroy Jesus from birth through King Herod. King Herod was disturbed when the Wise Men asked him, "Where is the one who has been born king of the Jews?" The Wise Men knew that Jesus was born because they saw Jesus' star when it rose and had come to worship Him (Matthew 2:1-2, NIV). In searching for Jesus to destroy His star or destiny, King Herod secretly met with the Wise Men and found the exact time the star had appeared. He sent them to Bethlehem and said, "Go and search carefully for the child. As soon as you find him, report to me, so that I too may go and worship him" (verse 7). One may ask the question, "why would a king be interested in finding a baby?" This was because Satan, who was behind Herod, knew who Jesus was and was aware of his destiny. In the correct context, it was an earthly king searching for the King of

Spiritual Warfare – Efforts To Destroy Our "Stars"

Glory (The King of all kings, Jesus Christ of Nazareth) to destroy Him before His kingdom manifests. Satan was aware that Jesus' kingdom would ultimately destroy his kingdom of darkness. The Wise Men followed the star they had seen until it stopped over the place where the child was. They were overjoyed when they could locate Jesus by the star's position. When they saw the child with His mother, Mary, they bowed down and worshiped Him. They also presented Him with gifts of gold, frankincense, and myrrh. They were warned in a dream not to return to Herod, so they returned to their country by another route (verses 7-12).

> *One may ask the question, "why would a king be interested in finding a baby?" This was because Satan, who was behind Herod, knew who Jesus was and was aware of his destiny. In the correct context, it was an earthly king searching for the King of Glory (The King of all kings, Jesus Christ of Nazareth) to destroy Him before His kingdom manifests. Satan was aware that Jesus' kingdom would ultimately destroy his kingdom of darkness.*

Baby Jesus was involved in an intense spiritual warfare between two kingdoms—the Kingdom of God and the Kingdom of Satan. Herod was on a mission to kill baby Jesus before His destiny would manifest. Herod was furious when he realized that the Wise Men outwitted him. He gave orders to kill all the boys two years old and under in Bethlehem and its vicinity in a concerted effort to kill baby Jesus. Satan's efforts through Herod failed. Jesus lived and fulfilled the will of God, the Father—lived a sinless life, died on Calvary's Cross, and was resurrected from the grave, thus actualizing the redemption plan for humanity. Jesus was God's rescue plan for humanity that Satan wanted to prevent from manifesting.

> Herod was on a mission to kill baby Jesus before His destiny would manifest.
> Jesus was God's rescue plan for humanity that Satan wanted to prevent from manifesting.

When the Holy Spirit leads us, nothing or no one can stop God's plan and purposes for our lives. We must trust in God, remain faithful and grounded in God's Word despite roadblocks, and walk in the path God sets. Satan made every effort to destroy my divine destiny. He tried to destroy my "star." However, to God be the glory, the light of God is reflected through me in this book and testimony. I am alive to tell the story of how God has brought me through. I am alive to tell others not to give up on themselves or their loved ones, no matter how bad things get. I am alive to tell people that when you do not understand what is happening in your life, trust God and His timing to deliver and heal you. God will protect you and fulfil the destiny He has preordained for your life.

> *When the Holy Spirit leads us, nothing or no one can stop God's plan and purposes for our lives.*
> *I am alive to tell others not to give up on themselves or their loved ones, no matter how bad things get.*

Witchcraft – Evil Forces Working Against Us

Witchcraft is an evil practice that connects with the spirit realm to manifest one's will in the earth. God explicitly condemns this practice in the Bible. In people's selfish pursuits for their will to be done, they have sought supernatural experiences outside of God's will. Those who practice diabolical witchcraft seek to inflict harm or even death upon others. They may also seek to thwart or destroy one's destiny and divine purpose. Various forms and/or tactics of manipulation and control were used as tools in witchcraft practices. God forbade occult practices in Deuteronomy 18:9-12 (NIV): "When you enter the land the Lord your God is giving you, do not learn to imitate the detestable ways of the nations there. Let no one be found among you who sacrifices their son or daughter in the fire, who practices divination or sorcery, interprets omens, engages in witchcraft, or casts spells, or who is a medium or spiritist or who consults the dead. Anyone who does these things is detestable to the Lord." God instructed the children of Israel not to indulge in various forms of occult practices that would defile them and invite Satan and his minions to infiltrate their lives. Witchcraft gives the enemy an open door to legally enter our lives, communities, and nations, ultimately destroying us. The penalty for practicing witchcraft under the Mosaic Law was death (Exodus 22:18; Leviticus 20:27).

> *In people's selfish pursuits for their will to be done, they have sought supernatural experiences outside of God's will. Witchcraft gives the enemy an open door to legally enter our lives, communities, and nations, ultimately destroying us.*

Another word that denotes witchcraft in the New Testament is sorcery. Sorcery is translated from the Greek word "pharmakeia," where we get our word pharmacy. Witchcraft often involves rituals using magic, incantations, and various drugs. The usage of illicit drugs can open doors for demonic spirits to invade our lives. Acts 13:6-7 mentions a sorcerer and false prophet named Bar-Jesus. The name Bar-Jesus means "son of Joshua" or "son of the savior." Isn't it ironic that the name of a sorcerer had a divine meaning? Satan often disguises himself as an angel of light—he appears to be something he is not. This is one reason why spiritual discernment is important for God's children. It helps us discern who is of God and the devil. The apostle Paul, filled with the power of the Holy Spirit, rebuked Bar-Jesus: "You are a child of the devil and an enemy of everything right! You are full of all kinds of deceit and trickery. Will you never stop perverting the right ways of the Lord? Now, the hand of the Lord is against you. You are going to be blind for a time, not even able to see the light of the sun" (Acts 13:10, NIV). Sorcerers and false prophets who pervert the way of the Lord must be exposed and rebuked to prevent their evil practices from further permeating society and even the church. After Paul rebuked Bar-Jesus, "Immediately mist and darkness came over him, and groped about, seeking someone to lead him by the hand" (verse 11). There are grave consequences for indulging in occult practices.

> " Satan often disguises himself as an angel of light—he appears to be something he is not.
> Sorcerers and false prophets who pervert the way of the Lord must be exposed and rebuked to prevent their evil practices from further permeating society and even the church. Satan's goal is to lure us away from worshipping God and turn to various spiritual powers outside of God's will. Any practice that taps into any spiritual source other than Jesus Christ of Nazareth is a form of witchcraft, no matter how innocent it may appear to be.

There are only two sources of spiritual power in the universe: God and Satan. God allows Satan to have power for a period of time, but ultimately, he will be completely stripped of all power. God allows Satan to have the power to test our faith so we can see where our hearts truly stand with Him. He also allows Satan to have power to demonstrate that His power is higher than Satan's. Those who engage in witchcraft seek to know the future and control events that they have no business controlling. In other words, they want to be gods. We should seek God's will to be done and not our own, trusting that God knows best in all situations and circumstances. Practicing witchcraft is a form of idolatry implying that we are "gods," thereby mocking God. The desire for us to be "gods" can be traced back to Satan's temptation in the Garden of Eden: "You can be like God" (Genesis 3:5). Satan's goal is to lure us away from worshipping God and turn to various spiritual powers outside of God's will. Any practice that taps into any spiritual source other than Jesus Christ of Nazareth is a form of witchcraft, no matter how innocent it may appear to be.

Spiritual Warfare – Efforts To Destroy Our "Stars"

> ❝ God allows Satan to have power for a period of time, but ultimately, he will be completely stripped of all power.
> God allows Satan to have the power to test our faith so we can see where our hearts truly stand with Him. He also allows Satan to have power to demonstrate that His power is higher than Satan's.
> We should seek God's will to be done and not our own, trusting that God knows best in all situations and circumstances.
> Practicing witchcraft is a form of idolatry implying that we are "gods," thereby mocking God.

God used my pastor, Windel Daley, and Apostle Christine Williams as vessels to facilitate my deliverance. Pastor Daley shared with me that he discerned that two witches were involved. Apostle Williams also confirmed and discerned the involvement of two witches. I was told that various evil spirits manifested, influencing me to do and say things. The demons used my faculties to speak through me. They were interrogated by the power of the Holy Spirit working through Pastor Daley. When Pastor Daley commanded the evil spirits to leave, they refused. He commanded them in Jesus's name to speak about why they could not leave. The demons explained that even if they wanted to leave, they could not leave because my ex-friend's mother, who is a witch, summoned them to torment me. They also said she buried two things in separate places I often visited to attach me to them, and they were sent with a purpose: to mad or kill me. When pastor Daley commanded the evil spirits to speak who sent them, the witch, through astral projection, presented herself and said, "I'm here; you can speak." According to the Merriam-Webster dictionary, astral projection is "the ability of a person's spirit to travel to distant places." When the pastor commanded the witch to leave me, or else he'd blind her or reverse what she did in the name of Jesus, she said she was not going anywhere until she fulfilled her purpose. She said I had potential, and she wouldn't allow me to come out better than my ex-friend.

> So much of spiritual warfare revolves around destroying or averting our divine destinies and purposes.

So much of spiritual warfare revolves around destroying or averting our divine destinies and purposes. It is imperative for us always to wear the full armor of God so that we may be able to stand against the wiles of the enemy (Ephesians 6:11-12). We are wrestling against spiritual wickedness in high places over our destinies (Ephesians 6:12). The Greek word for wrestle is "pale." According to Bible Study Tools, "pale" means wrestling – a contest between two in which each endeavour to throw the other and which is decided when the victor is able to hold his opponent down with his hand upon his neck. The term is transferred to the Christian's struggle with the power of evil." This brings to mind wrestling matches in the natural world. Both opponents struggle and tussle to pin the other to the ground. Whoever can hold the other on the ground for a certain period of time wins the match. As Christians, we may sometimes feel pinned to the ground by the adversary. However, we are not governed by feelings—we walk by faith, not sight. We understand that everything isn't what it appears to be. We are more than conquerors because He [Jesus] is greater within us than he [Satan] in the world. Jesus has conquered Satan! We already have victory in this wrestling match because of Jesus' victory on Calvary's Cross. Let us walk in this victory and trust God's process despite the circumstances or situation.

> *Jesus has conquered Satan! We already have victory in this wrestling match because of Jesus' victory on Calvary's Cross. Let us walk in this victory and trust God's process despite the circumstances or situation.*

"Don't worry. God is never blind to your tears, never deaf to your prayers, and never silent to your pain. He sees, He hears, and He will deliver."

-Unknown

Chapter 7

Journey of Mental Deliverance & Healing

The biblical difference between healing and deliverance is their distinct purposes and outcomes. Healing refers to physical, psychological, spiritual, or emotional well-being. In Psalms 147:3, David mentions God healing the emotions and the body: "He heals the broken-hearted and binds up their wounds." There was physical healing that Jesus and the apostles demonstrated in their ministries. In Matthew 9:35, Jesus demonstrated healing sicknesses and diseases among the people. Peter healed Aeneas, who was paralyzed (Acts 9:33-34). On the other hand, deliverance is the casting out of demonic/evil spirits or being set free from demonic oppression. Luke 8:2 records the account of certain women who were healed from evil spirits and infirmities and the casting out of seven demons from Mary Magdelene. In Luke 9:37-42, Jesus came to a boy who was in an epileptic-like state. "Then Jesus rebuked the unclean spirit, healed the child, and returned him to his father." So, we can see that God uses deliverance, the casting out of demons, to heal body, soul, and spirit.

It's natural to panic when adverse situations arise, as we perceive things are out of our control. Instead of seeking God, who has everything under control, we ultimately try to figure things out ourselves or run to someone or something that we think will give us quick solutions to our problems. Unfortunately, we leave God as our last resort when situations worsen. When nothing works out, we break down before God and wonder why He has not healed or delivered us. God then asks us, "Have you sought me yet?" God implores us to seek Him first (Matthew 6:33) because He knows what is best for us. God's will for our lives is better than our will for ourselves.

> God implores us to seek Him first (Matthew 6:33) because He knows what is best for us. God's will for our lives is better than our will for ourselves.

I believed and accepted that my situation was beyond scientific explanation. Psychiatrists and psychologists tried their best to work together to help restore or improve my mental health, but I progressively got worse. Recurring panic attacks, suicidal ideations and attempts, weight gain, memory issues, and even moving in slow motion, according to family members, were some of my symptoms. My situation was bigger than the resolution of human efforts, but it was not bigger than God, whom I know and serve. I started looking to Him for my healing and deliverance. I visited numerous churches seeking deliverance and attended several fasting services, crusades, and other services held at churches, hoping God would manifest His power of deliverance through one of His servants. As much as I wanted to attend church, I was uncomfortable being there. As a result, I tried to leave, experienced panic attacks, or had outbursts that drew attention to me, which disrupted services. I often wonder how being in the midst of worship and preaching could be a trigger for me.

> *My situation was bigger than the resolution of human efforts, but it was not bigger than God, whom I know and serve.*

I remembered attending a particular church, and to my understanding, I started to act in ways that disrupted the services. A church member told them to remove me so that church service could proceed uninterrupted. To my dismay, that was exactly what they did. I was not accepted or tolerated by every church I visited, which was very hurtful and disappointing. I think that not everyone could spiritually discern that I was undergoing special spiritual warfare that I later came to acknowledge. However, I grew to have confidence that God would deliver me. I visited several churches, and pastors consecrated olive oil and water and gave me to drink. After a particular pastor preached, he gave me the handkerchief he used to wipe his sweat and instructed me to bring it wherever I went so that no evil spirit(s) would come near me. I remember someone asking me, "What would have happened if I left the handkerchief one day at home?"

I recognize now that I lacked spiritual knowledge and understanding concerning this matter. What the pastor did was biblical because God's anointing flowed through the handkerchief of the apostle Paul. I believe the pastor was extending faith in God's anointing to do the same in my situation. Acts 19:11-12 states, "God worked unusual miracles by the hands of Paul, so that even handkerchiefs or aprons were brought from his body to the sick, and the diseases left them, and the evil spirits went out of them." It is imperative for God's servants to carefully explain what they are doing during deliverance so that our faith in God can be strengthened and supported by His Word. After the question was asked, I immediately felt fear hovering over me. I thought, "Am I supposed to bathe, sleep, and do everything with this handkerchief? Was I placing my faith in God or this handkerchief?" I later decided to throw it away. However, if I had proper teaching from the initial stage, I would have known that God could use His healing power through the handkerchief and perhaps receive immediate healing and deliverance if I had faith in God. The Bible didn't say that people had to walk around with Paul's handkerchief; rather, they received their healing immediately, and evil spirits left them.

> *It is imperative for God's servants to carefully explain what they are doing during deliverance so that our faith in God can be strengthened and supported by His Word.*

Spiritual persons would also tell me to put garlic under my tongue to experience healing and deliverance. I was told garlic is a protective element against evil spirits. However, I have learned that was a deception; it was rather supporting witches and demons. I was ignorantly idolizing and placing my trust in garlic rather than in God. This is a myth, along with burning frankincense in a place to repel evil spirits. When I bathed, I was told to throw a certain oil in my water to ward off evil spirits. Believing in these myths just opened spiritual portals, giving demons legal access to continue tormenting me.

> *Believing in these myths just opened spiritual portals, giving demons legal access to continue tormenting me.*

God isn't pleased with us practicing myths in our daily lives. Paul advised Timothy to reject profane and old wives' fables and to exercise yourself toward godliness (1 Timothy 4:7). According to Biblical hermeneutics, the Greek word used here is "mythos." It carries a negative connotation, characterizing beliefs as fanciful, untrue, and even deceptive. The devil is, however, the master of deception, leading people astray by turning them away from God. These myths were often employed to excuse immoral behaviors, which connote an intent of evilness or wrongdoing. Essentially, it refers to fictional fables lacking a solid foundation of truth. So, when Paul advised Timothy to avoid "silly myths," he was cautioning against indulging in baseless stories or fanciful tales. Conversely, Timothy is encouraged to focus on godliness and spiritual growth.

When persons around me recognized that I was not delivered after going to several churches, they suggested I sought a "mother," commonly known as an "obeah" woman. According to Giraldo, "the practice of "obeah" is the belief that one can use certain spirits or supernatural agents to work harm to the living, or to call them off from such mischief. The practice harnesses supernatural forces and spirits for one's personal use." Northeastern University posited two paths in the practice of "obeah:" (1) "supernatural realm," which "involves the art of casting spells, the warding off of evil, the conjuring of luck and wealth, and the protection of oneself and others" and (2) "medical authority" which "involves the knowledge and use of certain plants and animal products to heal illnesses." The persons who suggested I consulted this spiritual source of power were ready and willing to take me because they genuinely loved me and couldn't bear to watch me tormented and suffer anymore.

I understood that they, like myself, were getting discouraged. We needed immediate results. But I refused to visit those persons, choosing to believe as the Word of God instructed us in James 5:14-15, "If there is anyone among you sick, let him call for the elders of the church, and let them pray over him, anointing him with oil in the name of the Lord. And the prayer of faith will save the sick, and the Lord will raise him up. And if he has committed sins, he will be forgiven." I never once thought of seeking anyone else but God, no matter how unbearable the pain and discomfort. I thought to myself, "how can I fight evil with evil? Or how could I overcome evil through evil sources?" Romans 12:21 reminds us, "Do not be overcome by evil, but overcome evil with good." I believed only the power of God could truly have delivered me from demonic oppression.

One day, I was going to a shop in my community. As I walked there, I was tormented by the voices I heard in my mind. Despite that, I arrived at the shop and saw Pastor Windel Daley of the Ebenezer Open Bible Church. He greeted me with a hug, and I fainted. As a minister of deliverance, the anointing upon him caused me to fall to the ground immediately. He did not explain at the time what happened, but God had appointed and anointed him for such ministry, so he understood the spiritual warfare I was undergoing.

He later explained to my family that the situation I was going through was not normal. He repeatedly told them that I did not have a mental illness, but rather, I was under a spiritual attack. The enemy wanted it to manifest to make others think I was "mad," but that wasn't the case.

Nevertheless, I started attending church services at Ebenezer Open Bible Church, where I got saved, baptized and became a member. Like the story of the boy who had epilepsy (Matthew 17:14-20), Pastor Daley realized my deliverance would not come easily. He recognized that although God had placed an anointing upon him, he needed to spend more time with God to use him to deliver me. He explained that he wasn't the deliverer; Jesus Christ, through the Holy Spirit who dwells in him, was the source of power who delivers. Jesus equipped His twelve disciples with power over unclean spirits to cast them out and to heal all kinds of sickness and diseases. Matthew 17:14-20 explained a situation that they couldn't handle. Still, Jesus taught them how to gain victory: "And when they had come to the multitude, a man came to Him, kneeling down to Him and saying, 'Lord, have mercy on my son, for he is an epileptic and suffers severely; for he often falls into the fire and often into the water. So, I brought him to Your disciples, but they could not cure him.'" Then Jesus answered, "O faithless and perverse generation, how long shall I be with you? How long shall I bear with you? Bring him here to Me." And Jesus rebuked the demon, and it came out of him, and the child was cured from that very hour. Then the disciples came to Jesus privately and said, "Why could we not cast it out?" So, Jesus said to them, "Because of your unbelief; for assuredly, I say to you, if you have faith as a mustard seed, you will say to this mountain, 'Move from here to there,' and it will move, and nothing will be impossible for you. However, this kind does not go out except by prayer and fasting.'" Pastor Daley took the initiative to go on months of praying and fasting on my behalf.

When I was twenty years of age, God moved upon Pastor Daley's life in a powerful way that demonic spirits and witches were manifesting themselves through me during the majority of church services, including Tuesday fasting and Sunday services. Through the power of the Holy Spirit, he would command evil spirits to leave my life. Pastor Daley explained that whenever I screamed or vomited, it was demonic spirits leaving my body. I remember several times during deliverance service when I was physically tired, so I requested to be seated. I constantly asked for water as I easily got thirsty. Pastor Daley explained that demons were working on my body so that they could gain rest and strength. They were adamant not to depart from my body. I experienced God's healing power and deliverance at each service. I vomited for days; I even threw up the medications I was taking for schizoaffective disorder. At a particular service, the Holy Spirit told him that He was giving me my complete deliverance. I went to the bathroom, and my mother witnessed me passing faeces in the form of a snake. I received my complete deliverance! I have never experienced such joy in a long time. Glory be to God!

After deliverance, Pastor Daley explained Matthew 12:43-45. "When an unclean spirit leaves a man, he goes through dry places, seeking rest, and finds none. Then he says, 'I will return to my house from which I came.' And when he comes, he finds it empty, swept, and put in order. Then he goes and takes seven other spirits more wicked than himself, and they enter and dwell there; the last state of that man is worse than the first. So shall it also be with this wicked generation.'" He explained that the evil spirits departed for a season, so I must walk upright and allow the Holy Spirit to dwell in me so that I would give no space to the devil. He then instructed me to thank God for my victory as other church members rejoiced in thanksgiving with me.

I was so happy and grateful knowing God finally delivered me. God didn't fail me, and neither did He make me ashamed. I came off the medications, but after a few months, I felt like the spiritual attacks were returning. I started to experience panic attacks and anxiety again. At no point, I wanted to be alone. Once more, because of reoccurring symptoms of mental illness, my family thought it was best for me to go back on psychotropic medications that I had stopped taking. I didn't understand what was happening to me as I believed I was set free by the power of the Holy Spirit. I felt bound and defeated again, like I was going in a circle. I learned by experience that the devil and his agents do not give up easily. They are persistent and relentless in their pursuit to hold us bound and hostage. Pastor Daley explained that the panic attacks and the things I was doing were of myself as he didn't discern any evil spirits. He continued to explain, "They were mostly fleshly, cursing expletives, spitting in the face of God's manservant, etc., it was all you." I got upset when he said I was the one who was doing everything at that point. I wondered why I would put myself in such a predicament when all I wanted was to be free from it all and live a normal life. I later learned how this was possible through the power of the mind.

Brain activity exists in our subconscious mind, including thoughts and feelings we may not be aware of. The subconscious mind is so effective as it plays a fascinating role in our daily lives. According to John (2023), "The subconscious mind is programmed by our beliefs, thoughts, and experiences, often without us realizing it. Our emotions, habits, and behaviors also influence it. Each time we experience a particular situation, our subconscious mind creates a neural pathway associated with that experience, which becomes our brain's automatic responsive method to situations in the future. This is why habits and behaviors, positive or negative, can be difficult to break."

With this context, I understood that although God delivered me through my subconscious mind, I still operated the same way I did while I was under demonic influence. After three years of being afflicted by the enemy, my subconscious mind stored thoughts, feelings, memories, and automatic processes that operated outside of my conscious awareness. Many of our behaviors and habits are rooted in the subconscious mind. The subconscious mind operates like a well-rehearsed dance performed by our minds. It guides routine actions and responses based on learned patterns and pathologies. I got used to isolating myself at times, listening to sad movies and songs, and these things made me feel depressed. Unknowingly, I was feeding the bad habits and routines I had developed while evil spirits tormented me. Funerals and certain places were still triggers for me—I experienced anxiety and panic attacks in those places. I started to become fearful, and I no longer wanted to be by myself.

I am not sure if it was fear or the subconscious mind, but over time, something opened a spiritual portal that brought me back to a position where I was once again under demonic attack and influence. I thought I probably needed a change of environment to be at peace. I asked a close friend who remained by my side during my ordeal if I could spend a few days with her, and she agreed. However, one night, when she was not present, I felt tormented and started to hear voices of suicide. There was no physical support, but I managed to ignore them and sleep through the night. In the morning, when I awoke, I felt so depressed, as if I still wanted to end it all. I desperately desired for all the torment, depression, panic attacks, and voices to stop. I felt mentally and emotionally drained. I did not know what to do. I felt like giving up because I was so tired of everything.

I packed my belongings and texted a friend to tell her I was leaving. She asked me to stay until she got home, but I left anyway. Within the same minute, I reached out to another friend, Garrick Wanliss, who I knew cared for me and would always listen to me. I expressed myself to him, and he asked me to call his sister, Christina Williams, an apostle. I explained to Christina what I was going through and abruptly stopped. "It doesn't make sense for me to explain anything; you won't understand," I told her. She asked me where I was and if I could visit her immediately at her home in Clarendon. I hesitated, wondering if it would have made sense for me to go. I didn't think she would have understood my situation even if I explained. Moreover, I had a bag of belongings with me as I left my friend's house. Something in me said to go, so I told her I would come. She directed me and asked her husband to meet me at a particular point in order to guide me to their home.

I felt like I entered a different atmosphere when I arrived at Apostle's Williams house. She greeted me with open arms and a friendly smile, immediately making me feel comfortable and welcomed. She placed two chairs outside in a cool area where we sat and talked. Although I felt welcomed, I still believed it did not matter for me to explain what I had been through because she wouldn't understand. After explaining that to her, I remembered her exact words, "Try me." She then explained some things she personally had been through while growing up. Although I was going through a mental and demonic situation, I thought I was not going through anything compared to all she told me. From that point, I began to open-up to her. After summarizing what I had experienced, she asked me to give her a minute as she was going to say something to her husband. When she returned, she told me they would love for me to stay with them, then asked me if I would like to stay. I surely was not expecting that. Knowing my condition and that I was also suicidal, I wondered why they were willing to allow me into their home and around their teenage children. She told me she wanted to help me. I felt grateful for the kindness and love I immediately received from a stranger.

I happily agreed to stay and then informed my family where I was staying and with whom. Apostle Williams introduced me to everyone who was living in her household. God had not yet blessed them with a church building, so church services would normally be held in their living room. Persons from the area and other relatives would normally attend services. However, living in a household of constant prayer, worship, and Christian morals prompted several demonic attacks. Apostle Williams pointed out some belongings I needed to get rid of, such as jewelry binding me to demonic spirits. I stayed with them for three months before receiving my complete deliverance.

She told me she wanted to be a vessel God could use to deliver me from demonic attacks. She elaborated that she could discern the operation of witchcraft that was hindering the deliverance. So, she decided to go on prayer and fasting on my behalf. Prayer meetings were normally held on Thursdays in her living room. One night, after Apostle Williams and her family went to bed, she explained that her children ran and called her. They were frightened by a situation where they saw me beating myself on the wall. When Apostle Williams came and called me, she said she heard a change in the tone of my voice as I expressed, "this isn't Shannese," and I mentioned another name. She experienced a witch speaking through me, saying, "She can't live any longer; today, I'm going to kill or mad her because she wasn't going to allow me to turn out better than her daughter." She explained that the witch speaking through me was aggressive, angry, defensive, and said many expletive words. She was able to discern several spirits present through the power of the Holy Spirit. She and her husband, Pastor Kevin Williams, and others at the home prayed with me. When I screamed and vomited, she discerned some of the demonic spirits leaving, but I was not yet completely delivered. She continued to explain that after I regained a sense of normalcy, she noticed that I did not remember anything that took place. I was confused as I asked questions like, "What happened? Why were my clothes ripped up?" She comforted me by telling me not to worry as the Holy Spirit instructed her to tell me to stop taking medications because I was going to receive complete deliverance.

The next day, a convention was held at her home, where Rev. Retica was the guest speaker. During praise and worship, the spirit of suicide manifested itself through me. Apostle Williams explained that I took off quickly, and no one could catch up. I ran from her home towards the road with moving vehicles. They finally got a hold of me and brought me back to her home, prayed with me, and rebuked demonic spirits. They said I screamed so loudly, like never before, in a manner where the whole community heard it and was disturbed by it. But after such screaming, I received my complete deliverance at the age of twenty-one. Praise God! Persons, including myself, started to glorify God. I then testified. The Bible exhorts us that our spiritual victory should be testified about: "And they overcame him by the blood of the Lamb and by the word of their testimony, and they did not love their lives to the death" (Revelation 12:11). As I testified, I recall saying these very words, "enough is enough!" I told the devil, depression, anxiety, panic attacks, witches, mental illness, medications, and everything that afflicted me that enough was enough. Through the power of the Holy Spirit operating through the servants of God, I have received my complete deliverance, once and for all. I am set free!

> *Through the power of the Holy Spirit operating through the servants of God, I have received my complete deliverance, once and for all. I am set free!*

Journey of Mental Deliverance & Healing

Shannese celebrating her birthdays at ages 19, 21, and 23, respectively.

Shannese and her family.

Shannese and her close friends, Jason Mills and Kishanna Hyman, as well as sister, Shannel Jackson.

"Your mental illness is not your identity. Your identity is in Christ."

-Kay Warren

Epilogue

Overcoming Stigma Attached to Mental Illness

A sound mind is a stable, functional, and healthy mind. A healthy mind is linked to our attitude and outlook on life as believers. The Word of God encourages us to cultivate a healthy mind with positive thinking in alignment with God's truth. This change starts from the inside and then reflects in our behavioral patterns. Romans 12:2 confirms where changes begin: "And do not be conformed to this world, but be transformed by the renewing of your mind, that you may prove what is that good and acceptable and perfect will of God." Our attitude or intention changes once our mind is transformed or changed, resulting in changed actions and behaviors. Proverbs 23:7 states, "For as he thinks in his heart, so is he." This verse emphasizes the connection between our inward thoughts and outward actions. The Holy Spirit reshapes and transforms how we think and who we are.

Epilogue

> *A sound mind recognizes who we are in Christ and is not dependent on human wisdom and strength.*

A sound mind recognizes who we are in Christ and is not dependent on human wisdom and strength. The Bible encourages us to cast our cares upon Him, for He cares for us (1 Peter 5:7). God does not want us to be preoccupied with the cares of life and lose our identities in Him. He is always available to guide us and strengthen us along the way. Worry, anxiety, depression, and fear are negative emotions that drive us away from the abundant life God has in store for us. Whether the situation seems small or great, God desires us to have a peaceful mind focused on eternal hope in Jesus Christ. A sound mind is guarded by prayer through daily meditation on God's Word. The Holy Spirit works together with God's Word to change us. For this reason, the Bible encourages us to "take the helmet of salvation, and the sword of the Spirit, which is the Word of God."

A sound mind is derived from the Greek word "sophroneo," which is a compound word combining "sodzo" and "phroneo." The Greek word sodzo means to be saved or delivered. It suggests something that is delivered, rescued, revived, salvaged, protected, and now safe and secure. One expositor suggests that the word "sodzo" depicts a person who was on the verge of death but then was revived and resuscitated because new life was breathed into him. "Phroneo" carries the idea of a person's intelligence or total frame of thinking, including his rationale, logic, and emotions. It also refers to every part of the human mind, including all the processes that make the mind function and come to conclusions. When both Greek words are compounded, it paints a picture of exactly what God has done for me through the power of the Holy Spirit—a mind that has been delivered, rescued, revived, salvaged, and protected and is now safe and secure through Jesus Christ (Renner, 2024).

The process of a sound mind is based on divine wisdom and clarity that God imparts rather than subjecting ourselves to manipulation by fear. In 2 Timothy 1, Paul saw Timothy's timidity and wanted him to know that his fear was not of God. It was important for Timothy to know and understand that the source of his fear was not God. This fear was intended to stop Timothy from using his gifts to glorify God. In verse six, Paul writes to Timothy, "I remind you to stir the gift of God which is in you…" Fear is designed to rob us of God's gifts. The Greek word used for stir is "anazopureo," which means "to kindle afresh or to keep in full flame" (Guzik, 2018). The idea is to stir up a fire to keep our gifts burning bright and strong. If a fire is left unattended or neglected, it will burn out. God wants us to keep our gifts burning for him with a bold spirit.

Epilogue

> *It was important for Timothy to know and understand that the source of his fear was not God. This fear was intended to stop Timothy from using his gifts to glorify God.*
> *Fear is designed to rob us of God's gifts.*

Having and maintaining a sound mind requires recognizing what is of God and what is not. The spirit of fear that incapacitates and immobilizes does not come from God. However, reverential fear is different—it is a holy reverence for God. God is not the source or author of the spirit of fear that blocks us from using our gifts to glorify Him. Dealing with ungodly fear requires understanding what God has given us: a spirit of power, love, and a sound mind. The Greek word for power is "dunamis," which denotes the ability to perform. According to biblehub.com, "For the believer, this applies to power to achieve by applying the Lord's inherent abilities. Power through God's ability is needed in every scene of life to grow in sanctification and prepare for Heaven (glorification)." This is not a self-serving kind of power where we seek to please ourselves; it is a humble type of power expressed in how we love and serve others. A good example is Jesus washing His disciples' feet (John 13:1-11).

> *God is not the source or author of the spirit of fear that blocks us from using our gifts to glorify Him.*
> *Dealing with ungodly fear requires understanding what God has given us: a spirit of power, love, and a sound mind.*

The reference to a sound mind in 2 Timothy 1:7 has the idea of a calm, self-controlled mind and not a confused mind subject to panic. We must reject what is not of God (the spirit of fear) and humbly receive and walk in what He has given (a spirit of power, love, and a sound mind). Paul writes this to Timothy because the spirit of boldness matters to fulfil God's purpose for our lives. God's purpose is more than acquiring material things of the world or fulfilling our selfish desires; it entails using the gifts He has given us to bless others. This is how we glorify His name and advance His kingdom. At the age of nineteen, the enemy attempted to derail my life from God's purpose by attacking my mind. The enemy wanted to destroy the gifts God had given me. This book is a testament that he has failed and what he intended for evil; God is now using for good to bless many people. At age twenty-one, God restored my mind, purpose, and destiny through His Word and the power of the Holy Spirit.

Epilogue

> *God's purpose is more than acquiring material things of the world or fulfilling our selfish desires; it entails using the gifts He has given us to bless others.*

Science and Mental Illness

There is a scientific explanation of mental illnesses and remedies that medical doctors prescribe. While I am a believer in Christ and firmly stand on God's Word, I do not dismiss or ignore the scientific aspect of mental illnesses. There is a tremendous wealth of research and information regarding mental diagnoses and treatments that have advanced in the last several decades that are beneficial to us. From my understanding, balance is the key to understanding the mind from a medical perspective. It is often viewed that chemical imbalance in the brain is the cause of many mental illnesses. For instance, Castle Peak Hospital, the oldest and largest psychiatric hospital in Hong Kong, elaborates on how the treatment of mental illness works. They explained:

> "Mental illness is caused by damage to certain parts of the brain, resulting in disturbed functioning of the brain cells, such as abnormal transmission of chemicals among brain cells. Such disturbance inside the brain manifests as mental symptoms involving cognitive function, the content of thought, perception, emotion, behavior, and

biological function (e.g., sleep and appetite) and impaired overall functioning of the person—generally, psychiatric medications work by restoring the balance of chemicals in the brain. For example, an antipsychotic normalizes the transmission of a chemical known as dopamine and, therefore, makes delusion subside. Some medications might even promote the healing of the brain. For example, an antidepressant works by restoring the normal transmission of a chemical called serotonin among the brain cells and promoting the healing of damaged parts of the brain through a growth factor called brain-derived neurotrophic factor."

The psychiatrist at Mandeville Hospital recommended that I underwent brain scans, which came back normal, indicating that there was no chemical imbalance in my brain. Despite this, I was diagnosed with schizoaffective disorder. She adjusted the type of medication and the dosages I was prescribed. I experienced extreme panic attacks, anxiety, fainting episodes, and severe depression while taking prescribed medications. The psychiatrist pointed out that she was trying everything, but the medications were not as effective as they should have been. This medical analysis and conclusion beg one to think that an evil power source was behind the psychological attacks I faced. I firmly believe that demonic spirits were the source of my mental

Epilogue

attacks to destroy my God-given gifts and derail my divine destiny. The enemy wanted to use mental illness to destroy my star. According to Campbell-Livingston (2016), "Psychologists believe that mental illnesses such as schizophrenia are often misinterpreted as sudden changes in behavior caused by demon possession or the consequences of 'obeah.' I agree to some extent; some individuals experience a chemical imbalance in the brain, leading to strange thoughts, behavior, and changes in how reality is perceived through the senses.'" I maintain the belief that "obeah" was the means by which demons targeted my mind to destroy it.

> " The enemy wanted to use mental illness to destroy my star.

I believe that receiving medical attention does not demonstrate a lack of faith in God. Doctors are God's gift to us, as we were created as intelligent beings. Satan and his minions cannot create; they can only imitate. Only the triune God can create – He is the all-knowing, all-seeing source of everything, including science. However, healthcare professionals dedicate time and effort to learn how to create and prescribe medicines, and apply such knowledge and understanding towards physical healing in repairing our bodies. They should be treated with the utmost respect as those who help to care for people.

2 Chronicles 16:12 is often taken out of context to deprive an ill person of receiving the medical attention that he or she needs: "And in the thirty-ninth year of his reign, Asa became diseased in his feet, and his malady was severe; yet in his disease, he did not seek the Lord, but the physicians." The Bible emphasized how Asa bypassed God and went straight to physicians for physical healing; that was the severity of the issue. Even when visiting medical doctors, our faith is in God to heal and restore us, not doctors, who are vessels God may use. While we are on a medical note, if a person does not have diabetes, why should this person take medications for diabetes? If a person is not hypertensive, why should this person take medication for high blood pressure? Likewise, if a person does not have a mental illness, why should this person take psychiatric medications to treat mental illnesses? Mental illnesses should be viewed and treated as every other illness.

> *Mental illnesses should be viewed and treated as every other illness.*

It is important to note that Asa's disease was the result of his refusing to hear God's Word of loving correction through Hanani, the seer. He refused to rely on God in the face of threats against him. He also refused to rely on God regarding his diseased feet at the end of his life. Overall, the Bible maintains a

Epilogue

positive posture regarding the role of physicians and medical care. However, it is never wise to seek physicians in lieu of God. The correct order is to seek God's wisdom and guidance first, and then, if He leads us to healthcare professionals, we proceed prayerfully. We can trust God and see His hand move mightily through physicians when necessary. Theologian Charles Spurgeon notes regarding Asa's predicament:

> "It is not wrong to send for physicians, it is quite right; but it is very wrong to send for physicians in place of crying to God, thus putting the human agency before the divine; besides, it is very probable that these physicians were only heathenish conjurors, necromancers, and pretenders to magical arts, and could not be consulted without implicating the patient in their evil practices."

Furthermore, the physicians spoken of in this passage were probably Egyptian physicians who pretended to expel diseases by charms, incantations, and mystic arts. These were satanic mediums that were used for healing for profit.

> " It is never wise to seek physicians in lieu of God. The correct order is to seek God's wisdom and guidance first, and then, if He leads us to healthcare professionals, we proceed prayerfully.

A Higher Power

> If my sudden change after my nineteenth birthday celebration was not a result of a demonic attack and the effect of an evil altar through witchcraft powers, why did my deliverance through the power of the Holy Spirit supersede my symptoms thereby giving me complete deliverance and healing?
> I believe my testimony is evidence that the power of the Holy Spirit is greater than the forces of darkness and even more productive and potent than what medical science has to offer.

As you consider my testimony and experience, ponder this question: if my sudden change after my nineteenth birthday celebration was not a result of a demonic attack and the effect of an evil altar through witchcraft powers, why did my deliverance through the power of the Holy Spirit supersede my symptoms thereby giving me complete deliverance and healing? I believe my testimony is evidence that the power of the Holy Spirit is greater than the forces of darkness and even more productive and potent than what medical science has to offer. The deliverance and healing of my mind have led me through the power of the Holy Spirit to write this book. The mind once regarded as "mad" is the same one that wrote this book. As such, this book is another proof of the power of the Holy Spirit. To

Epilogue

God be the glory, I am not on any psychotropic medications presently, and the Holy Spirit enabled me to control my mind to pen these words. A higher power must have been involved in dismantling the powers of darkness used against me. Medical intervention did not save, heal, or deliver me, although that might have subsided my symptoms to an extent. A higher power got involved, and I received my complete healing and deliverance.

> " The mind once regarded as "mad" is the same one that wrote this book. As such, this book is another proof of the power of the Holy Spirit.
> A higher power must have been involved in dismantling the powers of darkness used against me.

The challenge between Elijah and the prophets of Baal revealed that the God of Israel was the true and living God (see 1 Kings 18:19-29). The prophets of Baal were shown that a higher power answered with fire and displayed unmatched authority. The Holy Spirit demonstrated a higher power against witches and evil spirits. It has been over three years since I took medications, or have experienced severe, moderate, or mild panic attacks, anxiety, fainting episodes, or severe depression. I have also lost between forty to fifty pounds as I went back to my normal weight before the attack and taking medications. Based on my medical history throughout this attack, doctors refused to accept that I was not mentally ill. I remember going to the hospital in 2023 because I was not feeling well. My symptoms included weakness, fever, joint pain, and reoccurring flu. Instead of the doctor listening to my complaint that it had nothing to do with mental illness, she looked through my docket file and asked me if I was still taking psychotropic medications. She then prescribed medications, requested blood tests, and wrote a referral for me to bring to the mental health clinic, stating that I was diagnosed with schizoaffective disorder and not currently on medications. The problem is that, at times, doctors fail to accept that the most profound truths are spiritually discerned rather than scientifically proven. As such, mental illness must be carefully examined through spiritual discernment.

> *At times, doctors fail to accept that the most profound truths are spiritually discerned rather than scientifically proven. As such, mental illness must be carefully examined through spiritual discernment.*

Epilogue

Spiritual Discernment

The gift of discerning spirits, or "distinguishing" spirits, is one of the gifts of the Holy Spirit described in 1 Corinthians 12:4-11. These spiritual gifts are given to believers for service in the body of Christ to reveal truth from falsehood. Spiritual discernment is a profound ability that transcends mere perception. It involves recognizing and understanding spiritual truths, distinguishing between good and evil, and grasping what may not be evident to the natural mind. Revelation is the mighty act of God whereby the Holy Spirit discloses to the human mind what could not be understood without divine intervention.

> *Revelation is the mighty act of God whereby the Holy Spirit discloses to the human mind what could not be understood without divine intervention.*

A discerning mind demonstrates wisdom and insight beyond what is seen and heard. For example, God's Word is "spiritually discerned." To the human mind without the Spirit, the things of God are "foolishness" (1 Corinthians 2:14). We ought to pray for the spirit of discernment to identify genuine people. "Beloved, do not believe every spirit, but test the spirits, whether they are of God because many false prophets have gone out into the world" (1 John 4:1). We must carefully examine persons we acquaint ourselves with to determine the level of trust we impart. As the Jamaican proverb goes, "A nuh every kin teet a laugh." Translation: Not every smile is a laugh. Meaning: Some people might smile and laugh with you, but they may not be genuine. The Bible admonishes us to trust in God and allow Him to lead our path to the people He wants to connect us with. Psalms 118:8 states, "It is better to trust in the Lord than to put confidence in man." The enemy will send persons into our lives to gain our trust and then use them to destroy us. David experienced and expressed his pain of betrayal from his acquaintance: "For it is not an enemy who reproaches me; then I could bear it. Nor is it one who hates me who has exalted himself against me; then I could hide from him. But it was you, a man my equal, companion, and acquaintance. We took sweet counsel together and walked to the house of God in the throng" (Psalm 55:12-14). After deliverance, I was advised to be alert and aware of who I eat from, whom I lend my belongings to, and from whom I accept things or money.

> We must carefully examine persons we acquaint ourselves with to determine the level of trust we impart.
> The enemy will send persons into our lives to gain our trust and then use them to destroy us.

Unfortunately, after my deliverance, the enemy attacked Apostle Williams and her family by getting evicted from their apartment. My screaming as the evil spirits were cast out was so disruptive to the community that they were asked to evacuate. This was a steep price they had to pay to engage in deliverance ministry and help me. They decided to move to Kingston, but I chose to return home to Manchester. Satan does not give up easily in his pursuit to destroy God's children and His purposes. Satan's attacks are persistently violent and relentless. For this reason, we must be persistent in our fight against the enemy by wearing the full armor of God and consistently engaging in covenant warfare prayers, reading, meditating, studying the Word of God, and fasting. I do not know if I could ever extend back such kindness to this family for the sacrificial love they have shared. I am eternally grateful to them for obeying the Holy Spirit and allowing Him to use them as vessels for my deliverance and healing. We remain in contact over the phone and share a wonderful friendship.

The enemy has robbed me of so much and caused me humiliation and rejection, even by schools. I did not let that hinder me from fulfilling my desire to return to school to pursue a career as a practical nurse. I was unsure where to start or what I wanted to do, but I saw how God worked it out for me to start nursing school. My mother sent me back to school as she worked as a domestic helper to help me complete a course in practical nursing at the National College of Professional Studies. During my journey of pursuing practical nursing, I recognized how much mental illness was stigmatized and discriminated against. The term "stigma" originates from the ancient Greek practice of branding criminals so that they were left with a mark (a stigma), which allowed them to be easily identified. The Merriam-Webster Dictionary (2012) defined stigma as "a) a scar left by iron, b) a mark of shame or discredit, and c) an identifying mark or characteristic; specifically: a specific diagnostic sign or disease." Persons with a stigma were devalued and rejected by society. Today, stigma refers to physical marks and any characteristic that sets an individual or group apart from mainstream society and "justifies" their disqualification from social acceptance and norms. People living with mental health conditions face discrimination as they experience barriers in looking for and keeping a job, safe housing, and health care services, as well as acceptance among peers at school. It also impacts social interactions with family members, friends, and the community.

I was flooded with a whirlwind of emotions when I returned to school. My determination to achieve, with the help of God and to put the enemy to shame, overcame all hindering negative thoughts and distractions. I dedicate time and effort to grasping

Epilogue

all theoretical and practical concepts. The enemy tried to discourage me along my journey, as persons within my community who attended the same academic institution circulated rumors about my past to my classmates, teacher, and principal. It was as if they underrated my ability to take on the coursework or to complete the program successfully. It was as if I was running a race with Shelly-Ann Fraser and Elaine Thompson, with spectators arguing that I was not qualified to be in their race. When the race began, they watched me to see me fall, to laugh, or to see me give up so they could say, "I told you so!" However, I knew the enemy orchestrated this, as they were ignorantly being used to discourage and hinder me from completing my race. But through endurance and perseverance, I believe I would complete my race.

> *Through endurance and perseverance, I believe I would complete my race.*

I did my working experience at Rock Garden Assisted Living, where I had to live for two weeks. I placed effort, passion, and care toward each patient. I completed each responsibility handed to me in a timely fashion with great pleasure. I ensured to pay keen attention to grasp the practical concept and apply it as I went along. During my training, I realized I had a deep passion to care for people. I automatically fell in love with my patients as they constantly placed a smile on my face. Due to this, I gained respect from my supervisor. A few days before my work experience was completed, my supervisor said, "I knew you before you got here." I became concerned, wondering what she meant by that. She elaborated by telling me that my classmates informed her that a female named Davidson was coming, and it would be difficult to accommodate me due to my constant fainting. This took me aback, as I recognized the enemy had gone ahead of me to plant negative expectations of who I was in the mind of my supervisor. She told me I had put them to shame because I'd done exceptionally well in my work experience, even better than those who spoke ill against my name.

> My supervisor told me I had put them to shame because I'd done exceptionally well in my work experience, even better than those who spoke ill against my name.

As time drew near to graduation in December 2021, I decided not to go, but my principal asked me to attend and offered to pay fifty percent of my graduation fee. I was so grateful and decided to go. On graduation, to my surprise, I was awarded the "Certificate of Appreciation in recognition of my outstanding contribution and dedication while completing my work experience at Rock Garden Assisted Living." I was also awarded

Epilogue

a certificate for "Outstanding Achievement for being the most outstanding student in best theory, best academic performance, and most discipline." I was so surprised and deeply moved by this as I reflected on my past, seeing how God had brought me a mighty long way. I have not only completed the coursework, I was also recognized for my outstanding performance. The final award that brought tears to my eyes was another certificate for "Outstanding Achievement for being the most outstanding student of the year 2021." Who could it have been but God? The principal, Mr. Dwayne Mckenzie, told me privately how much my name was brought to him as persons explained things that took place in my past, but he refused to accept or believe what they said about me. He expressed that he saw so much potential in me. God manifested success in this achievement, the very thing that the enemy wanted to rob me of in the past. The stigma attached to mental illness was trying to hinder God's purpose for me. Probably, if God had not delivered me from such, I would have developed low self-esteem, fallen back into depression, and ultimately just given up because society was fighting not to give me a chance. But the school's motto resonated with me, "I can do all things through Christ who strengthens me" (Philippians 4:13).

Both spiritual and medical recovery from mental health conditions is possible. However, stigma and discrimination often get in the way and prevent people from seeking and receiving the help and care they need on the way to recovery. The #DoYourShare anti-stigma campaign was an initiative officially launched in October 2022 to prioritize the creation of safe spaces for young people who may be struggling with mental health challenges. According to the Gleaner (2024), this campaign "is aimed at providing the platforms for people to share their stories and experiences of mental health disorders as well as access resources while reducing stigma." With this, I pray there will be more resources in Jamaica for public education on these matters to bring awareness to mental illnesses and remove stigma. After graduation, I worked at nursing homes in Manchester. In 2023, I heard there was a vacant position for a Community Health Aide within my community, so I applied in faith. A few months later, I was contacted for an interview, and within a few months after the interview, I received a call that I was among the few candidates selected as a Community Health Aide. I began my employment in October 2023 and am presently working there. Praise God! I am so grateful for this position. In addition, I am still a member of the Ebenezer Open Bible Church, where I was recently appointed assistant secretary.

Let me take the liberty of echoing this sentiment. The beauty of my testimony is that God used the same mind that the enemy tried to destroy to write this memoir. I see Genesis 50:20

Epilogue

speaking directly to me and my testimony, "But as for you, you meant evil against me; but God meant it for good, in order to bring it about as it is this day, to save many people alive." What the enemy meant for evil, my God has turned it around for my good so that I can testify of God's grace and mercy and the power of the Holy Spirit to deliver and heal from evil spirits. God has rescued my mind!

> " The beauty of my testimony is that God used the same mind that the enemy tried to destroy to write this memoir. God has rescued my mind!

Some of Shannese's church family at the Ebenezer Open Bible Church.

Epilogue

Shannese successfully graduating from National College of Professional Studies in 2021.

Shannese fellowshipping with Apostle Christine Williams in 2024 at The Way of Holiness and Deliverance Ministry.

Epilogue

Shannese receiving a membership certificate at the Ebenezer Open Bible Church from Reverend Windel Daley.

Shannese holding her awards with her former teacher, Mrs. Bartley, at her graduation 2021.

Declaration Of Truth

For those struggling with any kind of mental illness or disorder, it is important to see yourself as God sees you. Speaking positive words and what God declares about you over your life will help build your confidence, which will help in the healing process.

Replace the lies from the enemy with the truth from God. It is God's Word alone that can defeat the enemy's lies.

Say and believe in what God declares about you. Walk in your deliverance! Below are declarations you can speak over your life daily:

1. I am fearfully and wonderfully made for a purpose. (Psalm 139:14)
2. I am chosen, royal, holy, and God's special possession. (1 Peter 2:9)
3. I have the mind of Christ. (1 Corinthians 2:16)
4. I am the righteousness of God in Christ Jesus. 2 Corinthians 5:21

Affirmations

5. I can do all things through Christ who strengthens me. (Philippians 4:13)
6. God's plans for me are to prosper, not harm, to give me hope and a future. (Jeremiah 29:11)
7. I am more than a conqueror through Jesus Christ who loves me. (Romans 8:37)
8. The Lord is my strength and shield; my heart trusts in Him, and I am helped. (Psalm 28:7)
9. I surrender my anxiety to God, knowing His peace will guard my heart and mind. (Philippians 4:6-7)
10. I hear the voice of Jesus, my Good Shepherd, who leads and guides me with love. (John 10:14-15,27)
11. I will run to the Rock, Jesus Christ, when my heart is overwhelmed. (Psalms 61:1-3)
12. When my heart condemns me, I rest in God's presence, knowing He does not condemn me. (1 John 3:19-20, Romans 8:1)
13. I will not be afraid because God is right here with me, holding my hand. He will strengthen me and help me. (Isaiah 41:10, 43:13)
14. God has not given me the spirit of fear but of power, love, and a sound mind. (2 Timothy 1:7)
15. I shall not die but live and declare the works of the Lord. (Psalm 118:17)

16. Greater is He that is in me than he who is in the world. (1 John 4:4)
17. No weapon formed against me will prosper, and every tongue which rises against me in judgment will be condemned. (Isaiah 54:17)
18. I am not afraid of what anyone can do to me because I trust the Lord. (Psalm 56:3-4)
19. If God is for me, who can be against me? (Romans 8:31)
20. I am the head and not the tail; I am above only and not beneath. (Deuteronomy 28:13)
21. By His stripes, I am healed and made whole. (Isaiah 53:5)
22. I am free from sin. (Galatians 5:1)
23. I have the peace of God. (John 14:27)
24. I waited patiently for the Lord; and He inclined unto me and heard my cry. (Psalms 40:1)
25. He brought me up out of a horrible pit, out of the miry clay, and set my feet upon a rock, and established my steps. (Psalms 40:2)
26. He has put a new song in my mouth—Praise to our God; Many will see it and fear and will trust in the Lord. (Psalms 40:3-4)

Prayer For Those Struggling with Mental Illnesses

Life is unpredictable, and we don't know what we will encounter in life, but as long as we have you, Lord Jesus, we have hope to overcome. Your Word says in Hebrews 13:8, "You are the same yesterday, today, and forever." Lord, with my testimony, I remain confident in knowing that You are a God who still delivers, heals, and works miracles. I present all individuals who are struggling with mental illnesses before you. I pray for their healing and deliverance through the power of the Holy Spirit. Please send the support they need in every aspect of their life. Help them to be reminded that even if parents, siblings, or other relatives or friends forsake them, You will take care of them. Clothe them with Your love and let them experience Your peace that surpasses understanding. Help them to love themselves for who they are and believe that they are fearfully and wonderfully created, for marvelous are Your works. I speak life over death, happiness over sadness, laughter over tears, strength over weakness, peace over torment, faith

Prayer For Those Struggling with Mental Illnesses

over fear, and a good, healthy mind over mental illness in the name of Jesus Christ of Nazareth!

Whether by working through medications or miraculous healing, let Your will be done. Let your purposes and destiny for their lives be fulfilled. Give them power through the Holy Spirit to overcome obstacles in their path. I bind, paralyze, and victimize every spirit of suicide, fear, depression, and every force of darkness that is trying to control their minds and destroy their purposes in Jesus' name. I command them to leave in the mighty name of Jesus and go to dry places (Matthew 12:43). I come against the generational curse of mental illness; I break that generational lineage in the mighty name of Jesus Christ of Nazareth. Lord Jesus, surround Your people with Your angels and give them the strength to face each day. Restore joy, peace, and desires that please You and bring happiness to their souls. Restore their appetites for food if lost. I pray, O God, that no weapon formed against them shall prosper, and you shall condemn every tongue that rises against them in judgment. Lord Jesus, please remove discrimination and stigma from mental illness. Provide platforms and ways for the voiceless to be heard. I decree and declare that identities are restored. I release healthy and peaceful minds in the precious name of Jesus Christ of Nazareth. Amen.

Prayer of Salvation

"I firmly believe that the best thing that can happen to us in our lifetimes is to accept Jesus into our hearts as our personal Lord and Savior. I believe there is nothing more important than this, not career, family, friends, money, positions, reputations, titles, education, or accolades. With that said, I want to take this opportunity to extend an invitation to accept Jesus into your heart as your personal Lord and Savior. I can assure you that he is a faithful God who loves you deeply and wants the best for you—eternal life worshiping him. If you accept this invitation, please pray with me:

> *Lord Jesus, Christ of Nazareth, son of the Living God,*
>
> *I confess that I am a sinner who has sinned against you and others. Please forgive me of all my sins, iniquities, unrighteousness, and transgressions, whether conscious, unconscious, or subconscious in thought, word, or deed. I believe you are the son of the living God whom God the Father sent to die on Calvary's cross for the remission of my sins. You are the spotless, sinless lamb of God who takes*

Prayer of Salvation

> *away the sin of the world. You are the perfect sacrifice who atoned for all my sin, past, present, and future. I participate in the divine exchange—please take my sin and give me your precious righteousness. I understand that my righteousness in this life is regarded as filthy rags to you. I totally put my faith and trust in you no matter what happens in this life. My heart belongs to you. I accept your righteousness, grace, mercy, forgiveness, and favor. Thank you for choosing to shed your blood to redeem my soul. I love you, Lord Jesus. Amen.*

If you prayed that prayer, I encourage you to be led by the Holy Spirit to a solid Bible-believing church.

Despite our ongoing struggles between the flesh and the spirit, our sinful human nature and the divine nature, God is faithful to complete the good work he began in us (Philippians 1:6). He is the author and finisher of our faith (Hebrews 12:2). May God continue to shine his face upon you. "The Lord blesses you and keeps you; The Lord makes His face shine upon you and be gracious to you; The Lord lifts up His countenance upon you, and gives you peace" (Numbers 6:24-26).

I love you, my brothers and sisters in Jesus Christ" (JayQues, 2022).

Byers, A. (2022). *Freud's Theory of the Mind: Explaining Conscious, Preconscious, and Unconscious Thinking.* Retrieved from https://medium.com/@alexisbyers398/freuds-theory-of-the-mind-a3c920a6115b

Cleveland Clinic, (2022). *Nasogastric Tube: What it is, Uses, Types.* Retrieved from https://my.clevelandclinic.org/health/treatments/24313-nasogastric-tube#overview

Diaz, K. (2024). *The Meaning of Romans 8:7: What is the Carnal Mind?* Retrieved from https://lifehopeandtruth.com/life/blog/the-meaning-of-romans-8-7-what-is-the-carnal-mind/

Elwell, W. (1996). *Baker's Evangelical Dictionary of Biblical Theology.* Retrieved from https://www.biblestudytools.com/dictionary/altar/

Francis, K. (2021). *Over 1,000 Suicides in 19 Years.* Retrieved from

References

https://www.jamaicaobserver.com/2021/06/27/over-1000-suicides-in-19-years/

Giraldo, A. *Obeah: The Ultimate Resistance.* Retrieved from https://scholar.library.miami.edu/slaves/Religion/religion.html

Gifford, G. (2022). *Mind vs. Brain: Gaining Biblical Clarity on the Difference.* Retrieved from https://www.biblicalcounselingcoalition.org/2022/04/01/mind-vs-brain-gaining-biblical-clarity-on-the-difference/

Got Questions Ministries (2022). *What is the Mind, Biblically Speaking?* Retrieved from https://www.gotquestions.org/what-is-the-mind.html

Got Questions Ministries (2023). *How Can I have the Mind of Christ.* Retrieved from https://www.gotquestions.org/mind-of-Christ.html

Jamaica Gleaner (2023). *Jamaica's Suicide Count Jumps 26% in 2022.* Retrieved from https://jamaica-gleaner.com/article/news/20230808/jamaicas-suicide-count-jumps-26-2022

JayQues (2022). *Love Conquers All: An Unbreakable Spiritual Bond Between Two Generations.* Take Flight Publishing.

John Hopkins Medicine (2024). *Brain Anatomy and How the Brain Works.* Retrieved from https://www.hopkinsmedicine.org/health/conditions-and-diseases/anatomy-of-the-brain#:~:text=The%20brain%20is%20a%20complex,central%20nervous%20system%2C%20or%20CNS.

Kennington, T. (2024). *Surprising Things the Bible Says About Mental Illness*. Retrieved from https://www.biblestudytools.com/bible-study/topical-studies/surprising-things-the-bible-says-about-mental-illness.html#google_vignette

Mayo Foundation for Medical Education and Research (1998-2024). Retrieved from https://www.mayoclinic.org/diseases-conditions/mental-illness/symptoms-causes/syc-20374968

Mills (2008). *A butterfly Restored: Seven Keys to Experience Spiritual Transformation*. Xlibris Corporation.

Mills (2011). *A Butterfly Restored: Arise and Shine*. Tate Publishing and Enterprises LLC.

Ministry of Health and Wellness Jamaica (2020). Retrieved from https://www.moh.gov.jm/presentation/message-of-the-minister-of-health-wellness-dr-the-hon-christopher-tufton-world-suicide-prevention-day-working-together-to-prevent-suicide/

References

Mitchell, J. (2022). *The Carnal Mind vs. the Spiritual Mind*. Retrieved from https://southeastchurch.org/the-carnal-mind-vs-the-spiritual-mind-9-25-22/

National Institute of Mental Health. *Panic Disorder*. Retrieved from https://www.nimh.nih.gov/health/statistics/panic-disorder

Northeastern University (2024). *What is Obeah?* Retrieved from https://ecda.northeastern.edu/home/about-exhibits/obeah-narratives-exhibit/what-is-obeah/

Power of Manifest (2023). *The Subconscious Mind: Its Influence on Manifestation*. Retrieved from https://powerofmanifest.com/the-subconscious-mind-its-influence-on-manifestation/

Renner, R (2024). *What Does it Mean to Have a Sound Mind?* Retrieved from https://renner.org/article/what-does-it-mean-to-have-a-sound-mind/

Yeshuah (2024). *Healing vs Deliverance: Differences & Similarities*. Retrieved from https://yeshuahboyton.com/healing-vs-deliverance/#:~:text=The%20difference%20between%20healing%20and%20deliverance%20is%20that,can%20see%20Jesus%20healing%20people%20through%20such%20deliverance

Made in the USA
Columbia, SC
21 May 2025